Simply
*Be***YOU***tiful*

DISCOVER GOD, FIND YOUR TRUE IDENTITY, & HEAL FROM TOXIC CHRISTIANS

SHANNON D. HAIR

DEDICATION

To Kayla Rachael Hodges Burbage, my beloved daughter, Satan tried to take your life even before you were born, but God saved it. The intensity of attacks on your life speaks of the heavy anointing that will flow through you.

God's promise to me is that I will see you fulfill your purpose and destiny on this earth. I am so proud that with every sunrise you chose to face the new day. Nothing is wasted in God's Kingdom. It is your time to shine! You were born for such a time as this! No more delay. No more defeat. You are a daughter of the King, the Bride of Christ! I am overwhelmed that God chose me to be your mom. Part of your destiny is in your name, Pure Lamb! I love you!

A GIFT FOR YOU

Your choice to read my book is truly an honor.

As a token of gratitude, I have a special gift for you—*absolutely free.*

Connect to God Audio Teaching

One Teaching in the 8-Part E-course:
"Flip the Narrative of Shame without Hiding in Fear and Defeat."

Shannon D Hair

SIMPLY FREEDOM

www.simplyshannon.org

Simply scan the QR code below
to obtain your free gift!

TABLE OF CONTENTS

INTRODUCTION

Have you ever felt like the odd ball? Have you ever felt like you don't quite fit in? Have you ever felt excluded by the church? Have church tradition, continual obligations, and the unexhaustable list of "shoulds" left you heartsick? Do you long to have meaningful relationships, but fear others' judgment and criticism?

Are you hungry for an authentic relationship with God? How do you picture Him? Is He cold, strict, and unreachable? Do you feel buried under a pile of condemnation? Are there areas in your life where you feel that you'll never be able to obtain freedom? Friend, if you answered yes to any of these questions this book is for you!

My passion and purpose for writing this book is to bring hope and healing for Believers that have been rejected, wounded, and left for dead by those within their local church congregations. My story is about a woman who strived to fit into the box of religion but instead was suffocated by it. And just when I thought I was unable to take another breath, the love of the Savior broke through and revealed the difference between relationship and religion.

My desire is that through my story, you will see, like I did, what true love looks like.

God's love is full of truth, and it is His truth that sets us free. Unfortunately, so many of us live out the lies of the enemy as if they were God's truth. These lies cause bad fruit, struggles, failures, and emotional pain. Throughout this book, I will transparently share the very lies that had held me hostage. With every lie that God revealed, He handed me a key to freedom. Now, I hand those keys to you so that you, too, can unlock your heart to breathe again.

I want you to see how beautifully unique you are! The world needs you to rise up and take your place. Yes, there is a place for **YOU** in this world. Regardless of the pain that you have walked through, the rejection you have endured, or the hopelessness you may feel, God wants to wrap His loving arms around you and lead you to a life of wholeness filled with joy, laughter, and adventure. His desire is to redeem and restore you to your rightful place in Him.

Journey with me through the valley of toxic Christianity filled with religious fog, personal heartache, disappointment, disillusionment, masks, shame, and people-pleasing.

Together, we will travel to the green pastures of healing and freedom to become the authentic person God created us to be qualified, confident, and *"Simply BeYOUTiful!"*

MY STORY

Section 1

THE DAY EVERYTHING CHANGED
CHAPTER 1

H ave you ever had a defining day in your life? We use dates as a point of reference. Everything happened either before or after that day. For example, most Americans born before 1990 would agree that 9/11/01 was a defining day for our country. People are able to remember in detail where they were and what they were doing. It was a tragedy that struck our nation of which we are still feeling the aftereffects. I, too, have had my own personal tragic day that changed everything.

The night before everything changed, I was exhausted from staying up too late looking for answers after another confrontation with my strong-willed daughter. I didn't know it at the time, but I was at the end of myself. I had no answers; my hope was depleted. I was so weary struggling in every area of my life – even church left me feeling empty.

When my eyes popped open on Wednesday, May 19, 2010, I did not know that this would be the day everything changed. May 19, 2010 was the day my daughter left home in anger and rebellion. Oh sure, the pressure had been building for months. You would have thought that I would not have been caught by surprise, but I was. My daughter wanted to be free – no responsibilities – simply doing what she wanted when she wanted to do it.

To say I was undone when the door slammed behind her is an understatement. My beautiful, stubborn daughter left without warning. I begged her not to leave; I was not prepared to be an empty nester. I had no mental preparation to deal with the emotional trauma. When she walked out the door, she ripped out my heart and my identity.

Life events rarely happen the way we imagine. As my daughter was growing up, I always had this image of joy and celebration as she left home to embark on her own independent journey. Little did I understand that all of my personal struggles (insecurities, religious fog, fears) effected her as well.

"Alice in Wonderland"
As I watched the scene unfold, I felt lightheaded. In many ways, I felt like I was having an out of body experience, watching my life from someone else's eyes. The emotions

were simply too much to comprehend, let alone handle. As Anne of Green Gables would say, I was dramatically in the "depths of despair".[1]

Suddenly, I was feeling like Alice in *Alice in Wonderland* as she fell down the almost endless rabbit hole.[2] Nothing made sense. I was positively frantic. This could not be happening. As I watched my only child drive off, I started wailing. I'm not talking about just crying hard. I'm referring to the ugly cry to top all ugly cries! There were sounds that came out of me that I did not know a human could make! What's worse, I couldn't stop them. I was completely freaking out. A lifetime of deeply buried wounds erupted like a volcano when that door slammed shut. My heart simply couldn't bear another beating.

My husband was beside himself trying to calm me down. My uncontrollable behavior and hysterics scared the poor guy! For the first time in my life, my emotions refused to be reigned or controlled by someone else's will. There was no rational explanation for the way I was acting except that every hidden and hurtful thing inside of me was violently and unapologetically letting loose like a typhoon hitting shore.

---

[1] https://www.anneofgreengables.com/
[2] https://www.youtube.com/watch?v=Q93VrYOXSe8

What deeply hidden wounds am I talking about? A lifetime of rejection, shame, fear, insecurities, and worthlessness as well as the fear of not being enough for my very own daughter to love me. I wanted to die that day. In my mind, I had no reason to live anymore. I was emotionally bankrupt. My husband wanted to take me to the hospital to get me sedated. I could not be consoled nor did I want to be consoled.

In my heart, I believed that God had let me down. Everything was His fault. Why did He even allow me to be born? Oh, the thoughts that went through my mind! Nevertheless, even in the midst of intense pain and darkness, my personality kicked in. Sometimes the things we do or the words that come out of our mouths in desperate situations are absolutely hilarious! Without meaning to be funny at all, I sat up and started to rock back and forth from my fetal position on the floor. I looked up and saw a can of Cheerwine (a Southern soda) my daughter had left on the kitchen table. I kept thinking over and over, "Oh no, she's gonna get thirsty! She has nothing to drink." I started screaming repeatedly at my husband in complete seriousness, "She's gonna get thirsty! She has nothing to drink!" Mind you, my voice started out soft and rapidly progressed to an unnatural and painful pitch.

It really is a silly thought to have in the midst of everything that was going on; thinking back on it makes me roll my eyes at myself and laugh. As I tell the story now, I understand that it wasn't just the lack of a drink. I didn't know how she was going to have provision for anything in her unprepared state. Where was she going? Where was she going to sleep that night? How was she going to eat? Would she be safe? I couldn't call the police because she was of age.

Smothered Love

You may be thinking to yourself that this woman needs to get a grip on reality. Her reaction is a bit overboard. Had I been emotionally healthy, then yes, I would agree with you; unfortunately, I wasn't. The sound of the door slamming was like an alarm blaring begging me to wake up. This one event alerted my soul to the unresolved pain and trauma hidden deep within it.

I'll never forget the day I found out I was pregnant with Kayla. I was the happiest human being on the planet. My husband and I constantly rubbed my belly and talked to her. When I was a child I had a dream of the little girl I would have one day. I made sure my daughter knew that she was wanted, loved and valued. The problem was that she had become an idol in my life. My heart's desire was for family and nothing else. I had no other aspirations in life except to be a wife and mother.

As Kayla grew, I spent a lot of time with her, teaching her and taking her to church. I encouraged her to dream big and go after those dreams. I thought I was building her up and giving her confidence to become an independent and successful woman. From Kayla's perspective, the words were filled with pressure as if what I was speaking to her was something unattainable. She told me that I loved her too much! Is there such a thing?!?

What Led Her to Leave
Kayla and I had an amazing relationship until her junior year of high school, or so I thought. Nevertheless, I remember the exact day that there was a shift in Kayla's heart, and she began to rebel. (Before we delve further into the story, allow me to clarify. I am sharing the story from my perspective *with Kayla's permission.*)

The night before her junior prom, something traumatic happened. New information about her boyfriend brought a lot of emotional damage. My husband and I handled it the best we knew how. Looking back, I still don't know how it could have been handled differently. Nevertheless, Kayla resented the interference. From that point on it was like our daughter became a different person. Her true feelings about church and church people were made plain to us. She let us know the harm she experienced as she watched behind the scenes while I was on payroll at a church.

I urged her to talk to me, but her anger rejected my attempts. She looked at me with contempt and disgust; therefore, our relationship became a rollercoaster on unstable tracks. She had completely shut down emotionally. The incident that occurred the night before her junior prom was the beginning of the end – the season of tears that would lead to triumph had commenced.

THROUGH THE LENS OF RELIGION
CHAPTER 2

I was raised going to church every time the doors were open. My world revolved around church. There was no separation between home life and church life. My parents were actively involved in church; people who called themselves Christians surrounded me. These people shaped my view of God and His character.

I really enjoyed church as a child. We went to a Nazarene church. Every summer my sister and I would go to church camp. I loved camp! I gave my heart to Jesus as a child during church camp. Vacation Bible School was another wonderful memory about my childhood and church. My parents would go around the neighborhood picking up the kids who wanted to go with us. There would be so many kids in the back of my dad's truck that there was barely room to sit. We would sing songs, play games, and laugh.

While there are memories that bring joy to my heart, there are also memories that bring tears to my eyes. Like most people in the 1970s and 1980s, I thought that I had to go back to the altar every week to "rededicate" my life to Jesus. Somehow I had succumbed to a belief that I needed to beg God to love me and stay in my life. I watched as the adults at church would treat each other horribly in private, yet smile and act like everything was fine in the pews on Sunday. This confused me and caused me to wonder if God did the same.

Christianity as A Teen

We changed churches when I was in middle school. I can remember my sister was brokenhearted about leaving all her friends; I just didn't want to show any emotion at all. We left the Nazarene denomination and entered the Pentecostal denomination. I **accepted** Jesus while I was a Nazarene, but I **experienced** God when I became Pentecostal.

When I was 13, I received the Baptism of the Holy Spirit and began to pray in tongues. I really enjoyed it because I knew that the Spirit could pray through me and for me. Since I didn't know what I needed or how to put into words what I needed, I thought it was cool that I was praying the perfect will of God. Still, I lived my life half in the world and half in the church. I wanted only enough of God so that I wouldn't go to Hell.
#typicalteenager

Even though I was having amazing moments with God, in other areas my life was falling apart. I experienced sexual trauma at a young age. As a result, I became promiscuous. I learned to put on the mask, smile, and hide my true self – at church and at home. I was displaying what I had learned from the adults in my childhood: hide your true emotions and never rock the boat.

As I grew older, I hated that people thought I was beautiful; I hated my body. Fear and shame that resulted from traumatic experiences tormented me on a consistent basis. The Lord gave me a dream during my senior year of High School. In the dream, I was on stage before a huge crowd preaching and laying hands on the sick. There was an angel that whispered in my ear, and I repeated what I heard him say. I repented to the Lord for my promiscuous lifestyle and wanted to live my life for the Lord. That dream gave me something to hold onto, a reason to really live. I had found purpose. Shortly after sharing my dream, I realized I was pregnant. Immediately I was condemned and called a hypocrite.

The truth was that I had repented and wanted to serve God. Tragically, I was advised that God would never be able to use me; I had ruined my life. To cover my sin and shame, I had an abortion. Image was everything and had to be maintained – even at the cost of my soul. To make matters worse, someone very close to me told me that no man would ever want me or love me if they knew the things that I had done.

Christianity As An Adult

As an adult I had grown weary of church. Nevertheless, I continued to attend out of obligation; it was the "right" thing to do. My heart's desire was to serve God, but it's difficult when shame is a constant shadow.

Despite what I had been told, I got married a year out of high school. In 2020, we will have been together for 30 years. Before we married, I told my husband everything fully expecting to be rejected; nonetheless, he chose to love me. The good, the bad, and the ugly. He still wanted me.

Every princess wants her happily ever after; however, that reality is only true in fairy tales. Marriage is not the cure for any wound. I thought that because I was loved and accepted by my husband all the stuff deep down in my soul would just magically heal. I thought I was weak because I couldn't just "get over it". Four months into our marriage, we learned that I was pregnant. I gave my heart and soul to Kayla. Surely this was the answer to all my pain! For about five years, life was fulfilling. But then, the issues I had kept hidden deep within my soul began to surface. I did things that further wounded my soul and sabotaged my marriage. I realized that the things that I thought would take my pain away hadn't. About seven years into our marriage my husband and I sat down to evaluate our relationship. A pastor had advised my husband to leave me saying that I was a helpless cause, damaged goods, and he would be better off without me.

But God! Even in the midst of accusations, shame, judgment and rejection, God gave me a husband who would stand by my side. He refused to leave or abandon me; he refused to walk away. This man stood up for me and stayed by my side. It was undeserved. God was opening my eyes to see His love.

As an adult I served consistently in whatever church we were attending. If you can name it, I probably volunteered for it – from cleaning the church, running the computer in the sound booth, serving in the nursery, teaching children, teens and adults. I had a few experiences with the Lord, but something still felt like it was missing. Therefore, I went to more services and worked harder in the church to no avail.

Unqualified

As previously stated, I reached out to religious leaders for guidance when I was struggling. Unfortunately, we know that hurt people hurt people. So instead of demonstrating the love of God, I received judgment and condemnation. Their words were like knives shoved into my already bleeding heart: "No one will ever want you if they find out what you've done. Jesus will never be able to use you; you've ruined your life before it has begun. Well, you can serve God, but you won't ever be able to pursue your dreams, etc." These harsh words further confirmed my fears that I was unqualified to be someone God could use to make a difference in the world.

The reality is that I am not alone in my experiences. There are countless hurting people who have been further injured by those within the church. Many exit the church in worse shape than when they arrived. Instead of experiencing the love of God, I have heard multiple stories of people being advised to leave the church because of the sin in their lives. Some people are simply told that they don't fit in with that particular group of people; therefore, they feel uncomfortable and unwelcomed. The church was designed to be a place of refuge, safety, and healing; however, many have found it to be a place of disappointment and disillusionment.

Despite my discouragement with the church, I never considered walking away from church as a whole. I might have changed congregations, but giving up on God was not an option. Why? Because it was the right thing to do. Those who knew me in the past would never have guessed the pain that was buried in my heart. Like most good church folks, my smile never waned, and the mask never slipped. Exposure meant pain; experience taught me that. It was to be avoided at all costs.

Insecure, Unsure, and Anxious

As I transitioned from a teenager to an adult, I was insecure, unsure, and anxious. On the outside I was outgoing and laughed a lot; however, inside there was a deep sadness. I had times of deep depression as I just couldn't seem to shake off the emotional baggage. When I did share a little about what I was experiencing, the response would often be, "You've got the Word. Find a scripture and pray over yourself." When I was sick, I was told that I must have sin in my life. These things added to my shame, and I became a nervous wreck. Let's be honest. No one likes to be constantly criticized or made to feel they never quite measure up to others' standards.

Simply Ugly

My senior year of high school I was Homecoming Queen, Senior Class Beauty, 2nd runner up in my high school's beauty pageant, and Best Looking Senior Superlative. For a moment these titles made me feel as though I belonged and was accepted. Unfortunately, I never felt beautiful.

To me, beauty comes from the inside out. While there was beauty inside me, I focused more on the hideous things that had happened to me. I've always felt ugly. Or, should I say dirty? I cringed every time someone said, "Oh, Shannon, you are so beautiful!" I did not want to be noticed. After high school, I gained weight to hide the beauty of my outer appearance. I just wanted to be simply ugly.

INTO THE WILDERNESS
CHAPTER 3

After my daughter, Kayla, left, I went into a three-year depression. I was able to complete everyday tasks, but not much more. In the midst of trying circumstances, what we really believe surfaces. Unfortunately, not everything we believe is based on truth. Nevertheless, I was learning that God was more concerned about my heart and my true character. God's greatest desire is a relationship with us.

God speaks to each of us differently. Some people hear Him whisper words to their hearts. Some people see grandiose visions. Me – I hear God in many ways, but God really talks to me through movies. As I embarked on the path of healing, God used the movie, *The Matrix*[3] to help me understand what the journey would look like. I love how God relates to us personally and speaks the language we can understand to get His point across.

---

[3] https://www.imdb.com/title/tt0133093/

To over-simplify this complex movie, the Matrix is a place where people are hooked up to machines, and they are used as power sources. The people who are hooked up to these machines live their lives through their dreams. The main character, Neo, is connected to the Matrix as a power source. He has a nagging feeling that something is wrong with the world, and he believes a man named Morpheus has the answer.

When Neo meets Morpheus, he gives Neo a choice: Red pill or Blue pill. If he chooses the blue pill, he will remain in the Matrix in ignorant bliss. If he chooses the red pill, Morpheus will show Neo how deep the rabbit hole really goes. Neo chooses the red pill, which serves as a tracer so he can be found inside of the Matrix. When Neo is found, and wakes up in the real world, he sees all these cables attached to him. He goes into shock because what he thought was his life was a lie. He has a difficult time adjusting.

That's exactly how I felt when my daughter left. I was in my own rabbit hole of reality, and I was going to find out just how deep it went. Most of my life had been lived through a dream world, ignoring the traumas, wounds, and disappointments that had been buried deep within my soul. Now I was experiencing my own shock, as wave after wave of reality came crashing down.

My Journey Begins

When I finally finished crying and blaming everyone else, including God, I took a deep breath and knew I had two choices: 1) I could take the blue pill (so to speak), and stay bitter and turn my back on God; or 2) I could take the red pill (so to speak), be brave, look in the mirror, and face the reality of my soul. If I chose the second, I would be forced to take responsibility and allow God to heal me. It's a difficult thing to stop pointing fingers, to stop blaming everyone, and instead take a good, hard look in the mirror.

Facts were facts. We were a broken family. Obviously, "church" and following rules was not the answer. I read my Bible, prayed, served at the church, and all the other things you are supposed to do to be a successful and happy person without results. I knew there were some things blocking God from moving in my life; I just didn't know what those "things" were.

In all transparency, I was terrified of what I would see when I looked inside myself. However, God gave me courage knowing that no matter how long or how dark the tunnel, there was a light gleaming with hope at the end. If I did not choose to deal with the pain now, it would only get worse.

Holy Spirit gently invited me on a journey of self-discovery and healing. Though terrified, I chose to trust Him as He turned the spotlight on every dark and broken place in my heart – not to bring more pain, but to bring complete healing. God gives us free choice; all He needed was my "yes" to begin.

Into the Wilderness

The words spoken about and against me brought much hardship and even more failure into my life. No one offered to counsel me through my issues. These negative experiences confirmed my wrong beliefs about God. Quite honestly, I was afraid of God, and I didn't like Him very much. Admitting these things out loud helped me to heal. God already knew my heart; still, He kept proving His unconditional love to me even though I was unable to see it.

Because God loves us so much, He leads us into the wilderness. No one enjoys the wilderness experience. It's lonely. It's desolate. It's uncomfortable. Nevertheless, the wilderness is not a place of punishment but of promise. We find our promised land at the end of the journey. The Israelites began to take possession of God's promises after 40 years of walking through the desert learning to depend on God for every need. For me, I wandered through the wilderness for seven years. I thought this wilderness was the effect of my brokenness. I wish I could say that I was able to withstand every test that came during this time, but I can't. What I am grateful for is that when I failed the tests, God revealed the lies I was embracing. When we believe a lie, we live it out as though it were truth. My early experiences in the church displayed a god that is not at all like Father God.

In the 1980's, there was an American female gymnast named Mary Lou Retton. At four years old, she dreamt of being a gymnast. At seven years old, she watched Nadia Comaneci compete in the Olympics and win. After that, all Mary Lou wanted was to stand on the podium and receive a gold medal. It was her dream. But dreams require much more than thoughts; true dreams require action. May Lou went into strict training in order for that dream to come to pass. She did the hard work that it took to make her dream a reality.[4]

As Mary Lou's gymnastic skills increased, she outgrew her coaches. Soon she was coached by the very couple that trained Nadia Comaneci. She spent grueling hours every day focused on her dream.

---

[4] http://www.encyclopedia.com/people/sports-and-games/sports-biographies/mary-lou-retton

Throughout the process, Mary Lou trusted her coaches and listened to their instructions. She imagined herself with the Gold Medal as the Star Spangled Banner played in the background. She visualized herself as a winner. People may come into our lives for a season, and their role is vital to our development. However, not everyone is meant to be in our lives forever. We must learn to discern when the time is right to step away and move forward. If we don't, we stifle our own growth.

Six weeks before the Olympics, Mary Lou got injured and needed surgery on her knee. Most of us would have given up and waited another four years for the next Summer games. Not Mary Lou! She remained focused on her dream. Mary Lou endured and pressed through every obstacle to get to the 1984 Summer Olympics. The pain was worth it! Mary Lou was the first American woman to receive a Gold Medal in gymnastics.[5] The time between the inception of the dream and its realization was years! It was a time of testing, developing, training and enduring. It was a time of preparation. Remember, anything worth having rarely comes easy.

Jesus Experienced a Wilderness
Even Jesus had to experience time in the wilderness.[5]

---

[5] Matthew 4

The Spirit of God led Jesus up into the mountains for 40 days to fast and pray. Imagine how weak and hungry Jesus may have been! We complain about three-day fasts! After 40 days, Satan visited Jesus to tempt Him. Isn't that just like the enemy to come at us when we are at our weakest and most vulnerable? Satan questioned Jesus' identity three times, aiming to get Jesus to falter.

Satan first tempted Jesus with food. He said, "If you are the Son of God, tell these stones to become bread".[6] Notice Satan said "if." He was attacking Jesus' identity and using food as the arrow because Jesus was hungry. Most of us would have been hangry!

Secondly, Satan tested Jesus by twisting the Word of God. "'If you are the Son of God,' he said, 'throw yourself down. For it is written: 'He will command his angels concerning you, and they will lift you up in their hands, so that you will not strike your foot against a stone.'"[7]

Psalm 91 does declare that God will give His angels charge over us; however, Satan's aim was to get Jesus out of alignment with His identity and purpose. If the angels had come when Jesus was on the cross, we would have been doomed for all eternity. So, before Jesus' ministry

---

[6] Matthew 4:3
[7] Matthew 4:6

began, Satan was trying to get Jesus to choose comfort over destiny.

And lastly, Satan offered Jesus a counterfeit destiny. "The devil took him to a very high mountain and showed him all the kingdoms of the world and their splendor. 'All this I will give you,' [Satan] said, 'if you will bow down and worship me.'"[8] Satan wanted Jesus to worship him instead of the Father.

In each instance, Jesus used the Word authentically and accurately against Satan. He withstood every test and temptation that was thrown at Him. When Jesus walked off that mountain, that place of testing, He was strengthened. He had endured, and now, He was ready to begin His public ministry.

---

[8] Matthew 4:8-9

THE ROAD TO HEALING
Section 1

TOXIC CHRISTIANITY
CHAPTER 4

Toxic Christianity sounds like an oxymoron; unfortunately, it's more prevalent than we'd like to admit. Before we gain insight into toxic Christianity, let's look at how the Bible defines Authentic Christianity:

"'Love the Lord your God with every passion of your heart, with all the energy of your being, and with every thought that is within you.' This is the great and supreme commandment. And the second is like it in importance: 'You must love your friend (neighbor) in the same way you love yourself.' Contained within these commandments to love you will find all the meaning of the Law and the Prophets."[9]

Toxic Christianity lacks one key word in the scriptures above: LOVE. Personally, I define toxic Christians as spiritual bullies who use the Bible (and even so-called "prophecy") as a weapon of destruction rather than

---

[9] Matthew 22:37-40 TPT

healing. Many believers who claimed to love me used the Word of God as a boxing glove leaving me bruised, battered, and bleeding. Just like the Pharisees in the days of Christ, toxic Christians are wounded people who struggle to love themselves; therefore, they are incapable of loving others as described in Matthew 22. They know the Scriptures, yet use them to their personal advantage, not for their personal transformation.

I absolutely love people. The truth is that we cannot give out what we do not possess. Therefore, it is difficult for people to love others if they do not love themselves. There was a time in my life when I couldn't love others in a healthy manner because I had no love for myself. I believed the lies that were said to me as well as the lies spoken about me. Now, I have a passion for all believers to be healed from damage caused through toxic Christianity.

Honestly, there is enough truth in religion to make it sound holy, righteous, and good. This is what makes it difficult to recognize at times. I'll be the first to admit that I'm not perfect! Jesus displayed immense patience with me as He taught me the difference between being an authentic Christian and doing church culture. Jesus was and is all about people and relationships. He is very clear that He will leave the ninety-nine to find the one.[10]

My prayer throughout this book is to illuminate truth and strategies God gave me to heal and to become an authentic Christian. God led me on a journey of discovering the TRUTH of His Word as He stitched the wounds that were inflicted upon me using distorted Bible verses. Scripture was never intended to control, manipulate or shame anyone. That is an abuse of the Word of God. The Word of God is a sword, an offensive weapon given to us to fight against spiritual dark forces.[11] But too many times we use it against each other, not the enemy of our souls!

The truth is that I became the very thing I despised: a toxic Christian. How can that happen? It was all I knew; unfortunately, it is the underlying culture of many of our churches today. I have walked through my fair share of hurt and rejection from toxic Christians, and I know that I am not alone in my journey. I have watched too many people walk away from the church shaking their heads with feelings of defeat and even disbelief. Those who came to the church for healing left limping with increased injuries. With heavy hearts and heads hung in

[10] Luke 15:4
[11] Ephesians 6:17

shame, these wounded ones exit the very place that was designed to be a source of love and safety.

I ask as you read this book that you look in the mirror of your own heart and ask God to show you yourself. Allow Him to heal every hurt and lonely place and to show you who He really is – His real, authentic, genuine self. God wants you to believe the truth about Him! He wants to burn away every lie that the enemy has used to build a wall between you and Him. You are the joy that was set before Jesus that empowered Him to endure the cross! You! Yes, you! He gave His life to have a relationship with you; therefore, He is passionate about revealing Himself to you! While it can be difficult to look into the mirror of our hearts, it is so worth it! I had to shake off wrong thinking and embrace the truth of a relationship with Jesus. I had to choose to live as He created me to live, not how someone else thought I should live.

Each of us has been hurt at some point in our lives; it's part of life. At the same time, if we are willing to be truthful, we have hurt others as well. We have all worn the label of a toxic Christian. It's important to understand that the majority of Christians are not toxic intentionally! We tend to want people to be just like us instead of celebrating the unique design God created them to be.

Jump outside the box of religion; see what you will find in the playground of relationship with Jesus! Without a change of mind, there can be no change of heart. Jesus lived outside the box. Yet, Christian culture has diluted the potency, intimacy and complete freedom found in walking with Him. Jesus is full of personality. He is fun! He is completely involved in every aspect of our lives where we allow Him access. Jesus is no different today than He was while walking on this earth.

God is moving in a fresh new way that no one has ever experienced. God is calling us back to His heart to have a personal, one on one, relationship with Him. God wants to restore, redeem and rebuild our lives! He desires for us to find our purpose and place in His Kingdom. God has not forgotten you. He created you first and foremost to have intimacy and relationship with Him; nevertheless, He also wants to see you surrounded by people who will love you, encourage you, and fight the enemy alongside you. This is where you fit; this is your tribe.

If God can do it for me, He can do it for you. This is exciting news! The winds of change are here. Jesus has heard your cries. He is answering those desperate cries whispered in the darkness. He has seen your pain. Jesus has never turned His back on you. You ARE good enough! You are WORTHY of His attention and love. He left the 99 to find you in your obscurity. He is calling you out of isolation. It's time to come out of the cave and back to His heart living the life you were designed to live – secure in your own unique beautiful identity!

GOD TAKES OUR WOUNDS SERIOUSLY
CHAPTER 5

God takes our wounds, our pains, and our tears seriously. Not one tear has escaped His notice. We wander around aimlessly in life and don't know which way to turn. He found me; He has found you. The Psalmist wrote, "You've kept track of all my wandering and my weeping. You've stored my many tears in your bottle—not one will be lost. For they are all recorded in your book of remembrance."[12]

I have heard too many stories where damage has been done in Jesus' Name. There were numerous instances when toxic Christians would quote scripture to manipulate, control, or shame me. I even had someone scream and throw the Bible at me while I was dealing with the trauma of my teenage pregnancy. The wounds of those words went deep, and the shame went even deeper. This pain was buried deep in my heart because facing the pain was more than I could handle. When my daughter left, all the memories from the past exploded,

---

[12] Psalm 56:8 TPT

giving me no choice but to acknowledge my pain. I often wonder how I was able to function as a normal human being despite the suffering in my soul. Those who knew me would never have guessed the things hidden in my heart.

I needed help! Each time I reached out to someone to help me, it seemed things got worse instead of better. How do you process the inner turmoil when you can't find a safe, judgmental free environment? But God is always faithful. He is Jehovah Jireh, our provider. When I started to understand that God wanted to deal with me on an emotional level, God sent me two precious friends. God brought them into my life for the season of healing. Slowly, I learned that I could be real and trust them. When wounds are ignored and left unattended, they fester; they don't die. God takes our wounds very seriously. That's why Jesus came to heal our wounds.

"For I will restore health to you, and I will heal your wounds, says the Lord, because they have called you an outcast, saying, This is Zion, whom no one seeks after and for whom no one cares!"[13]

---

[13] Jeremiah 30:17 AMPC

God wants to restore our hearts and reintroduce Himself to us in personal ways. My life has been transformed by a personal relationship with Father God. He wants that for you too! There will always be opportunities on a daily basis to become wounded and offended. Life happens, but God has taught me to no longer bury or deny my emotions. Now, I run into the safe arms of my loving Father and give my wounds and hurts to Him, allowing His love to bring the healing that I need. I no longer focus on things of the past. I turn my eyes to His love and choose to look for the victories in my life. I no longer hide from Him because of the imperfections in my life. God loves us as we are in the moment we are. God doesn't see us as broken people. He sees us as whole because Jesus took our brokenness. "But he [Jesus] was hurt because of us; he suffered so. Our wrongdoing wounded and crushed him. He endured the breaking that made us whole. The injuries he suffered became our healing."[14]

Wounded Soldiers

One day I was talking to God about people who were wounded by toxic Christianity. I knew I wasn't the only one, and others have far worse stories than mine. God gave me a vision of Christians dressed as soldiers.

---

[14] Isaiah 53:5 VOICE

Normally, soldiers cover each other in a battle and pull the wounded to safety. Once they are safe, doctors come to dress and bandage the physical wounds of these soldiers. After they have been treated, the soldiers are moved to a recovery room to heal.

In the vision, I saw Christians in a raging war with bullets flying everywhere. As I looked at the battlefield, I saw bodies covering the field with blood. When the battle ceased for a moment, many were lying on the ground crying out for help. Some were wounded worse than others. But not everyone was knocked down. Some soldiers were still standing. I wept as I saw the majority of the standing soldiers kick and walk away from those crying out for help. As these soldiers turned their backs on the hurting and walked away, disdain covered their faces. I was horrified as in the vision some of the soldiers reached for their guns and shot those who had been injured during the battle. Others would just look the other way, pretending that those on the ground were not there because they didn't know how to help them. Some soldiers simply ignored the wounded because their own comfort was their highest priority. It would have been inconvenient and uncomfortable to help those damaged by the war. I began to cry out to the Lord for help.

The Lord told me to look again. As I continued to survey the battleground, I noticed a few soldiers displaying mercy and compassion toward those who were in great pain. Then I saw angels coming to aid the soldiers who ministered healing to the wounded.

When the vision ended, tears streamed down my face. I knew what it felt like to be lying on the ground reaching out looking for a helping hand. I believe the Lord was giving me a visual of what a portion of the Body of Christ looks like today – hardened soldiers who have no tolerance for pain or weakness or who are consumed with their own comfort and needs. God said that He hears the cries of the wounded, and He answers their prayers for help. In this next season, angels will have a huge role in ministering to those on the battlefield as well as those in the recovery room.

I don't know where you are in your life. You may feel as though you are doing well, yet have a lot of anger and bitterness towards the church. I understand! But know this: God sees all. He is not ignorant, nor does He bless the actions of those who hurt His sheep. Our Father is a good Shepherd, and to those who have the opportunity to help and don't, He says:

"You have not strengthened the weak or healed the sick or bound up the injured. You have not brought back the strays or searched for the lost. You have ruled them harshly and brutally. So they were scattered because there was no shepherd, and when they were scattered they became food for all the wild animals."[15]

"Therefore this is what the Sovereign LORD says to them: See, I myself will judge between the fat sheep and the lean sheep. Because you shove with flank and shoulder, butting all the weak sheep with your horns until you have driven them away, I will save my flock, and they will no longer be plundered. I will judge between one sheep and another."[16]

"I will place over them one shepherd, my servant David, and He will tend them; He will tend them and be their shepherd. I the LORD will be their God, and my servant David will be prince among them. I the LORD have spoken."[17]

---

[15] Ezekiel 34:4–5
[16] Ezekiel 34:20–22
[17] Ezekiel 34:23–24

We are created to love and to be loved. We were never created to be tolerated and/or bullied by those around us. We need companionship and friendship in our lives. Through my own journey, God connected me with healthy Christians who helped me in my journey. They were safe, and their love enabled me to be transparent. I used to think it was impossible to remove the mask and allow others to see my brokenness, shame, and heartache. We need people in our lives with whom we can be our authentic selves. If you need safe people in your life, ask God to reveal to you with whom in your life you can be real and raw. He often connects us with the right people at the right time. It is in experiencing love through vulnerability that we experience new waves of His love towards us.

As my heart began to heal, I made a conscious effort not to talk about the negative experiences. I did not go to God and make a long list of their shortcomings, nor did I ask God to fix them. Instead, I made a choice to forgive those who had hurt me and asked God to forgive me for the things I said or did to hurt others. Then, I asked God to bless and have compassion on those I had forgiven because God had given me so much mercy and compassion in the midst of my own sin.

But let's be honest, before I gained healing I had quite A LOT to say to God about the people and situations! But I've since learned that when we go to God and act as the accuser, the lawyer, and the judge, we pronounce verdicts on others that hinder God from moving in their lives as well as ours. Judgment and accusations originate with Satan. He is the father of lies, and the accuser of Christians.[18] When we accuse others, or even ourselves, we are under Satan's influence.

Lord, forgive us for the judgments we have made regarding those who have hurt us! Forgive us for the judgment and accusations we have made against ourselves! Work in us and through us to heal our wounded souls in Jesus name!

---

[18] Revelation 12:10

A FRESH LOOK AT SALVATION
CHAPTER 6

I t doesn't take an expert to see that the majority of our American churches lack authenticity. People are leaving churches by the masses. People come for love and healing yet leave more wounded than when they arrived. I'm not trying to sound harsh or critical, but I believe God is getting ready to radically change church in America.

In 2015, I decided to take a sabbatical. I began to pray in earnest to discover how I could have an active role in assisting those who have been impacted by toxic Christianity. I didn't want to GO to church anymore; I wanted to BE the church.

Unfortunately, the church as we currently know it in Western culture has real issues! Some days it feels as though it will be impossible for the church to change, and some people don't even want the church to change! But we serve a God of the impossible. The church is supposed to be the Bride of Christ, but the majority of church-goers are not acting very bride-like. I love the way the Passion

Translation describes the relationship between husband and wife.

"And to the husbands, you are to demonstrate love for your wives with the same tender devotion that Christ demonstrated to us, His bride. For He died for us, sacrificing himself to make us holy and pure, cleansing us through the showering of the pure water of the Word of God. All that He does in us is designed to make us a mature church for His pleasure, until we become a source of praise to Him—glorious and radiant, beautiful and holy, without fault or flaw.

"Husbands have the obligation of loving and caring for their wives the same way they love and care for their own bodies, for to love your wife is to love your own self. No one abuses His own body, but pampers it – serving and satisfying its needs. That's exactly what Christ does for His church! He serves and satisfies us as members of His body.

> "For this reason a man is to leave His father and His mother and lovingly hold to His wife, since the two have become joined as one flesh. Marriage is the beautiful design of the Almighty, a great and sacred

mystery—meant to be a vivid example of Christ and His church."[19]

Jesus loves the church, His Bride. He is serious about tending to her wounds. Each of us has a vital part in what God wants to do in this hour. We are not supposed to live in isolation rehearsing our wounds. We are created for relationship. In order to enjoy relationship as God designed, we need to be willing to let God heal our souls. I promise it is possible.

Every Christian is part of the body of Christ; therefore, we need to love each other. If we stub our toe, causing pain, do we chop off our toe? No, we nurse the pain. If you're like me, you'll act like it's the end of the world, over-exaggerating the pain. God wants to heal us so that we can walk in authority and victory in every situation. As we learn to do this, we are becoming His pure and spotless Bride. While there is much change to be done, it always begins with one person. Are you willing to be that person?

In order to walk in complete victory, we need to see the big picture. Let's start with salvation. Most people are taught to say a sinner's prayer to keep them from going to Hell. With this type of heart attitude, we are only trying

_____

[19] *Ephesians 5:25-31*

to figure out what God will tolerate and still allow us into Heaven. We want just enough God in our lives to stay out of Hell. We don't really care if God loves us or has plans for us; we just want to live our lives according to our desires. This lifestyle is referred to as lukewarm, and it brings nothing but misery. Can this attitude even be deemed as "saved"? Does this sound like a bride getting ready for her marriage?

Generally, people think salvation is "Eternal Fire Insurance" or a "Get Out of Hell Free" card. Salvation is so much more! The Lord showed me that Jesus' death and resurrection brings complete deliverance to spirit, soul, and body – physical as well as emotional healing! His purpose was not just to save us, but also to give us the authority to rule and reign on this earth. When we choose to believe that Jesus Christ is Lord, the Holy Spirit takes up residence within us. The same power that raised Jesus from the dead lives in those who have received salvation. Most people don't realize that "Resurrection Power" is part of what Jesus purchased for us.

How exciting is that? The **exact** same power that raised Jesus Christ from the dead lives within us! Unfortunately, in many Christians this power lies dormant – untapped and hibernating. The author of Hebrews reminds us that we are heirs of salvation. As such, we receive a divine inheritance as God's kids. God longs for each of His sons and daughters to bring heaven to earth and to enjoy every benefit of being His child in the here and now. The Father values each of us so much that He paid the highest price possible – the sacrifice of His only Son, Jesus.

One Greek word for salvation is σωτηρία "soteria." It is a noun meaning, "deliverance, preservation, safety, salvation."[20] Jesus offers us protection in every area of life; however, we choose His protection by allowing Him access into every area of our lives. Through the death and resurrection of Jesus Christ, God gave us an all-access card into Heaven. All the benefits of Heaven are available to us now; however, relationships are two-way streets. Jesus wants us to spend time with Him and get to know Him. Guess what else? He wants to get to know us! Even in natural relationships, we can't know someone by reading about them or by what someone else says about them. How do we get to know the people in our lives that we are close to? We spend time with them. We ask them questions. We learn what they like or dislike. We learn what makes them laugh and what makes them cry. When we know someone really well, they don't even need to speak. We can read their actions.

---

[20] *https://www.biblestudytools.com/lexicons/greek/kjv/soteria.html*

Jesus compared His relationship with the Church to the relationship between husband and wife. Imagine a healthy marriage. What would happen if the couple stopped talking after they got married? There wouldn't be a marriage. It sounds ridiculous doesn't it? What if our spouses gave us the silent treatment for the rest of our lives?

Jesus wants to talk with us! He wants to talk to us like we talk to our friends. He talked to Abraham, Moses, and Joseph. These men were not prophets. They were humans just like you and me. God's character never changes! He created humans to have relationship and conversation with Him. When we spend time with Him, we fall in love with Him. We think about Him. We get to know His likes and dislikes. This is part of the awe factor. The creator of the universe sees us as His bride. He loves us so passionately that He looks forward to spending time with us. Maybe this hasn't been your experience, but it can be!

We all have people in our lives that only show up when they want something. It's aggravating, isn't it? They don't really care about you personally; they just want what they can get from you. Jesus is not a Sugar Daddy. True love seeks relationship for what can be given, not received. Truth be told, for most of my relationship with the Lord, I would only talk to Jesus and beg Him to help me out of situations. For example, I would pray that my daughter would quit rebelling, or ask for help when our finances were short. I rarely took the time to just BE with Him.

Jesus displays His unfailing love for us in a multitude of ways every single day. The problem is that we are too blinded by pain and offense to see it. But there is hope! Through intimacy with Him, the blinders are removed; we are able to see and experience His love. Intimacy with God cost Jesus His very life. He values what He paid for. Jesus paid the highest price for us. Shame can't keep Him from loving us. Sin can't keep Him from loving us. Nothing in Heaven, earth, or below the earth can keep Him from loving us.

"But [you were purchased] with the precious blood of Christ (the Messiah), like that of a [sacrificial] lamb without blemish or spot."[21]

"Since we are now joined to Christ, we have been given the treasures of redemption by His blood—the total cancellation of our sins—all because of the cascading riches of His grace," (Ephesians 1:7 TPT).

---

[21] 1 Peter 1:19 AMPC

What does redemption mean? "In theology, the purchase of God's favor by the death and sufferings of Christ; the ransom or deliverance of sinners from the bondage of sin and the penalties of God's violated law by the atonement of Christ."[22] What does redemption cover? To put it simply, it covers whatever we need – every pain in our spirit, soul, and body. It covers our sorrows, toxic shame, depression, anxiety, heartache, regret, molestation, rape, mental abuse, sexual abuse, spiritual abuse, physical abuse, emotional abuse, and so much more! Redemption restores us back to the original person of health – mentally, emotionally, physically, and spiritually. For years, I thought the cross was only for our spirits, not our bodies and souls. Thankfully, Jesus came to redeem our spirits, our souls (mind, will, and emotions) and our physical bodies.

Our sins are washed away in the blood of Jesus, and He has made us kings and priests to God.[23] Everything that God does in the earth He does through His sons and daughters. As Christians, we are no longer simply an earthen vessel, but a heavenly being living on the earth. Jesus gave us authority to rule the world and bring it into alignment with heaven. We are a royal priesthood. Royalty carries a kingly anointing, and priesthood carries

---

[22] http://webstersdictionary1828.com/Dictionary/redemption
[23] Revelation 1:5-6

54

a spiritual anointing. We are called to go into the presence of God and come back in strength with a strategy. Unfortunately, many Christians are not taught that God wants to truly partner with them on the earth. They are taught to simply attend church on Sunday morning, give their 10% (or more) every Sunday, and do their best to live a moral life. Our world has been suffering while we have been sleeping in ignorance.

During a conversation with a girl I was mentoring, I gave her a practical illustration regarding salvation. I told her a story about a man who had saved some money and bought a ticket to board a ship to come to America. He had brought along a little bit of food to get him by until he arrived at his destination. However, the man never took the time to research what benefits were included with his ticket. He just assumed it was for the passage. The man stayed below deck in his cabin until the last night of the voyage. He had decided after a long journey that he would splurge on a nice dinner, and then he would walk around the boat and enjoy the ocean breeze while looking at the stars sprinkled across the sky. During dinner, one of the waiters commented that he had not seen the man during the trip. The man explained to the waiter that he had brought food with him that lasted him through the passage, but wanted to celebrate the last night as he had a little bit of money. The waiter asked,

"Sir, did you not realize that all the food, beverages, and entertainment were included in the price of your ticket?"

Emotional Healing

God created us with a spirit, a soul (mind, will, and emotions), and a body. In order to gain complete wholeness, we need to receive healing in our spirit, in our soul, and in our body. We learn about repentance and how to take care of our spirits in church, but we often neglect our mind, will, and emotions. Tragically, a lot of churches don't even believe in healing anymore. They teach that Jesus puts sickness on people to teach them lessons. The devil is a liar!

When I was in my early 20's, I remember going to the altar and crying all the time. If you asked me why I was crying, I wouldn't have been able to tell you. I just knew my heart was hurting. The pastor prayed for me repeatedly and finally said, "Shannon, I just don't know what to do for you." The poor guy was genuinely perplexed, and honestly didn't have the answer. He didn't say this to embarrass me or hurt me; however, due to my deep brokenness, I was left with a deeper sense of shame. I felt I was so defective that even Jesus couldn't help me.

But God is faithful! As I learned to do more listening and less talking at God, He began to teach me about emotional wounds and trauma. A soul wound is an emotional hurt that has not been addressed or healed. These can include any kind of trauma, inner turmoil, bad betrayal, anger issues, and anxiety to name of few. The behavior is a lot easier to identify than the root cause of the behavior. There were wounds in my life that had never been addressed – going all the way back to childhood.

While we can ignore or suppress these traumas in our lives, they still show up in our behavior. For me, my relief came through escapism. My methods were binge watching TV or movies, romance novels, eating, and living in a fantasy world. There are plenty of things we can do to escape emotional pain to try to keep it at arm's length. Some other forms of escapism are drinking, pornography, retail therapy, or drugs.

Another sign that we need inner healing is the feeling that "nothing is ever good enough." That was a big one for me too. In church, all I ever learned was to pray, quote scripture, and stand in faith. I did these things because that was what I was taught to do. Truthfully, I felt like I was blindfolded playing "Pin the Tail on the Donkey." I was just hoping to hit the bull's-eye and that by some sort of luck my faith would "work".

Disappointment from doing what I was told to without results caused me to believe the lie that Jesus wasn't true to His Word. Maybe it would work for someone who is worthy, but it wasn't working for me. I was desperate for freedom, but the freedom I needed seemed to elude me. My heart was filled with agony as I felt like a freak that Jesus couldn't help. It wasn't until God revealed to me that Jesus cared about my emotional wounds that I saw hope for lasting freedom.

When we have wounds in our soul, this opens the door for demonic spirits to torment us. These are landing strips that give the devil access into our lives to create even more problems. Once we acknowledge and recognize we have a soul wound, we can begin the healing process. And here's the truth: Jesus really does care, and He loves to trade! Our pain for His healing! Our wounds for His cleansing blood. Our torment for His peace. Healed soul wounds are included in our salvation package! We just need to know how to access this healing and apply it to our lives.

The problem with emotional pain is that it's not easy to deal with. When we have a physical sickness, we go to the doctor and discuss the symptoms. We get the medicine we need to feel better. If we break our arm, we wear a cast for a number of weeks. If a physical wound takes time to heal, then emotional wounds do too. The severity of the trauma will determine the length of time it will take to heal. But in our society (and even in some churches), we are taught to cover the pain rather than expose it.

Some of my soul wounds healed instantly while others have been a process with layers of healing. The longer process of healing usually came when I had built a wall of protection around an area of my life to protect myself from further pain. The Holy Spirit would knock down one brick at a time until I was free.

I used to get angry with God when He walked me through a process. I expected instant freedom. The waiting made me wonder if God could be trusted. I was so afraid that He was prolonging the healing to make me suffer. Now I understand that it is through the process that character, strength, and endurance are built. Through it all, I have learned things that have helped me to pursue my dreams. God **can** be trusted! God is always working for our good; therefore, we can rest and trust Him even through the pressure of the process. God's desire is for us to prosper, be healed, and whole.

SHANNON D. HAIR

"Beloved, I pray that you may prosper in every way and [that your body] may keep well, even as [I know] your soul keeps well and prospers."[24]

Sin and trauma cause wounds to our soul. Merriam-Webster defines sin as:
    a) an offense against religious or moral law
    b) an action that is or is felt to be highly reprehensible
    c) an often serious shortcoming : fault"[25]

Sometimes these come from those who have sinned against us; other times they come from our own sin. Our soul processes and stores everything that comes against us. This comes through our mindsets, thoughts, attitudes, emotions, feelings, and beliefs. Every aspect of our life is touched by what is in our soul. Wounded souls can cause illnesses within our bodies over time. When we are born again, our spirit man is made perfect. Nonetheless, we still have a soul that has not been perfected.

We can compare our spiritual rebirth to a natural birth. You wouldn't expect a newborn baby to immediately start running. No, babies have to develop and mature.

---

[24] 3 John 1:2
[25] https://www.merriam-webster.com/dictionary/sin (accessed 1/14/19)

60

Spiritual growth takes time as well. We have to allow ourselves the process of getting our souls healed as we grow in the knowledge of who God is. Many churches focus only on the spirit and expect people to be perfect immediately after they receive Jesus.

Just like a child, we have to learn the character of those around us. God is good. It is not just a trite saying; it is the true character of God. God loves you; God loves me. God is not ashamed of either of us. Even though people may reject us, Jesus never will.

THE CHURCH IN ACTS
CHAPTER 7

Getting the Most Out of Our Tickets
Just like the man on the boat who had an all-inclusive ticket; salvation is our ticket to receive every blessing that Jesus purchased. Jesus paid our debt in full. Our salvation not only gives us eternal access to Heaven but also authority to agree with Heaven on the earth. We have been given the power to overcome obstacles. Loving Jesus doesn't stop trial or tribulation, but it does give us the knowledge that whatever we face we win! This knowledge doesn't come magically. We need to be intentional about developing our relationship with God.

Too many people say, "If it's God's will, He will heal me." It is always God's will to heal. The cross of Christ included healing; it was a package deal with forgiveness of sins and entrance into Heaven. There is never an instance where Jesus *refused* to heal. There were times when He could not heal, like in His hometown. It's not that He didn't *want* to heal. He *could not* heal because the people in His hometown did not believe.[26] God's desire is to heal everyone – body, soul, and spirit! Jesus may have used different methods of healing for each person, but they were healed. When our prayers aren't answered, we blame God. But what if there is a spiritual law in operation that is the true hindrance?

God is good. He is not the author of suffering. Study Jesus' life, and make your own decisions. The more I read about Jesus, the more I see His heart to heal and to help all who ask. God doesn't send storms into our lives; He calms them.[27] God doesn't put us in painful situations to teach us lessons. That wouldn't be considered good; it would go against His character. We tell Jesus to leave us alone, get out of our governments, and get out of our schools. If Jesus leaves, who is left? The devil; he is the enemy of our souls, and he comes to steal, kill, and destroy.[28]

As we read the book of Acts, we get a glimpse of how the early church looked and operated. One thing I noticed was that the church in Acts didn't have ridiculous displays of creativity to keep people's attention. Don't get me wrong, flashy lights and other things are cool, but they seem lame in comparison to the power and

---

[26] Mark 6:4-6
[27] Luke 8:22-25
[28] John 10:10

presence of God. Are we going to church for entertainment or encounters with God? Do we want to be amused for a moment or transformed for a lifetime?

So what did the early church look like, and why is it important? Why were they experiencing the power of God, and why aren't we? The early church was devoted to His Word, prayer, taking communion and fellowship. "They devoted themselves to the apostles' teaching and to fellowship, to the breaking of bread and to prayer."[29]

The early church was in love with the written word. The apostle's illuminated how Jesus fulfilled the prophecies written in their Holy Scriptures. There was no printed Bible, and the letters they received were actual letters rolled up like scrolls. They invited the Holy Spirit to breathe on the words and bring fresh understanding and revelation. We call the collection of books and letters the Bible. We believe that it is the living Word of God, full of energy and can pierce more sharply than a two-edged sword. It can even penetrate to the very core of our being where soul and spirit, bone and marrow meet.[30]

The early church was devoted to prayer. Do you wonder what they were praying for? Do you think they were

---

[29] Acts 2:42 NIV
[30] Hebrews 4:12

asking God for more money, better jobs, and bigger houses? Too often we have a list of what we want from God, and after we have checked off our list, we walk away. We don't take the time to hear what He may want to say to us. True prayer is a conversation between Jesus and us. But because we don't stop to listen, we beg Jesus to hear us. We simply don't have the confidence that intimacy brings.

But the apostle John encourages us, "This is the confidence we have in approaching God: that if we ask anything according to his will, he hears us. And if we know that he hears us—whatever we ask—we know that we have what we asked of him."[31] Let me keep it real: when I first started reading my Bible and praying at home, five minutes was agony for me. Five minutes felt like FOREVER! As my relationship with Jesus grew and my religious duty waned, I found that the minutes flew by!

The early church regularly took communion. Jesus wants us to honor and celebrate His blood and His body. When we take communion we are retelling the story and proclaiming the Lord's death and resurrection until He comes.[32] Don't look at this through religious eyes. This is

---

[31] 1 John 5:14-15
[32] 1 Corinthians 11:17-34

an intimate moment between Jesus and us. When Jesus took the cup, He said it was for the forgiveness of sins and to establish the new covenant. "In the same way, after the supper he took the cup, saying, 'This cup is the new covenant in my blood, which is poured out for you.'"[33] Communion has become a regular part of my time with Jesus. I especially enjoy taking communion with my loved ones. There is an intimacy that is so beautiful when we come to God's table together. By honoring Jesus' body, we are also honoring one another. Communion is a time to receive Christ's forgiveness and to forgive those who hurt us. It helps us to move forward with clean slates walking in God's mercy. Remember, you can't love God and hate your brother or sister.[34]

What does it mean to have fellowship? Is it really eating a fried chicken dinner with macaroni and cheese after church? A good example is actually a gang. Why? Gang members are known for their loyalty to each other, and they are willing to protect and fight for each other. They are often together; they live and love each other like family. They live by a certain code. If we take out all the bad stuff from gangs, it is very similar to what true fellowship is. The gang acts like family without being blood-related. Each member is initiated into the gang.

---

[33] Luke 22:20
[34] 1 John 4:20-12

We are adopted into the family of God. Oh, that we would learn to love and honor one another! Jesus said, "A new command I give you: Love one another. As I have loved you, so you must love one another. By this everyone will know that you are my disciples, if you love one another."[35]

---

[35] John 13:34-35

THE TRUE HEART OF GOD
CHAPTER 8

Show Me the Father

God worked patiently with me when my daughter left home. I told the Lord that I wanted to scratch everything I knew about Him and start fresh. I wanted to learn who He was through my own studies and personal experiences with Him; I no longer wanted to rely solely on what others have told or shown me.

"Jesus explained, 'I am the Way, I am the Truth, and I am the Life. No one comes next to the Father except through union with me. To know me is to know my Father too. And from now on you will realize that you have seen Him and experienced Him.'

"Philip spoke up, 'Lord, show us the Father, and that will be all that we need!'

"Jesus replied, 'Philip, I've been with you all this time and you still don't know who I am? How could you ask me to show you

the Father, for anyone who has looked at
me has seen the Father."[36]

Distorted View of the Father

How do we get such confusing and controversial views
about God? I had formed opinions about Him through my
personal experiences with Christians who were harsh,
judgmental, and cold. I read the Bible through the lens of
what I was told to believe as well as through the actions
of toxic Christians. In my heart I knew that something
was amiss: The Jesus in the Bible was not the same Jesus
that I saw in Christian culture.

You would have thought that after decades of church, I
had a healthy view of God, but I didn't. I decided to study
the life of Jesus. The scripture clearly states that if we see
Jesus, we see the Father. Jesus perfectly imitates the
Father. Here's the problem: If we have had bad
experiences with other Christians, it only confirms and
backs up beliefs that God is distant and mean. How would
we know that what we believe is false? Truthfully, I was
afraid of God for most of my life. In my mind, He was
sitting on the throne in Heaven with a belt in His hand,
ready to strike at the least infraction. Not only did I fear

---

[36] John 14:6-9 TPT

Him, but I didn't like Him all that much. I just didn't want to go to hell when I died.

We often view God by how our earthly fathers act and react. My own dad worked hard, provided well for us, took quality time to spend with us, and carved out time every summer to take us on vacation. He was a kind and generous man who would help anyone in need. He made sure that I knew right from wrong and took me to church every week. My dad was a great man; his life impacted so many others for the good. As wonderful as he was, there were times when my dad could be harsh or critical. His standard was so high at times it felt unattainable. Therefore, I began to believe that while God was kind and generous, He was also critical with impossible standards. This is why Satan targets fathers, marriages and families. Relationship is at the very core of who God is. It is the whole reason He created human beings in the first place.

The church also plays a large role in how we view God. Unfortunately, there is a performance mentality in the Church. If you perform and meet the status quo, you are accepted. If you do not, you are considered an outcast and kept at arm's length. As visitors, we are warmly welcomed; as members, we are worn out striving to maintain the religious rules and obligations of the church. These further enforce the lies that we have to earn God's love, and that God is a harsh taskmaster who can't be pleased.

The Devil is a Liar

You've probably heard it. You may have even said it, "The Devil is a liar!" In order to keep us from drawing near to God, Satan does His best to distort our view of God's true nature through bad experiences. It's important to understand where deception originates. Satan hates God passionately; he tries to hurt God through stealing people's identities, killing their faith and trust in God, and destroying their lives in whatever way he can.

My senior year of high school was full of conflicting emotions! It was the most difficult and traumatic time of my life as well as amazingly adventurous and full of fun. These contradictory messages were completely typical in my life. At this time, my mom was searching and learning about spiritual things. She attended a church revival service, and the preacher talked about the devil and demons. I distinctly remember my mom saying one time, "Bring it on, devil." While she said it in naiveté, she also adamantly believed in the power of God. Well... the devil brought it.

Both of my grandfathers passed away that year as well as my cousin who was only three months younger than me. Emotionally, I was spent. What little I had left, I used to stuff down some of the unspoken traumatic things that were happening to me. At the same time, we began to encounter demonic activity in our home. Before cell phones, when there was only one phone line in the house, the phone would ring between 2:00 – 3:00am on school nights. When we answered, the voice sounded like one of my deceased grandfathers, and then would rapidly turn into ear-piercing shrieks. All kinds of strange things were happening, and I was terrified!

While I was dealing with my own issues, my mom about had a nervous breakdown, and I was trying to take care of her. Evil was on the loose, and it felt just as powerful as God. I became very angry with God. I blamed Him for all the evil we were facing. I missed a lot of school that year. I thought if I backed off from God, then the demonic activity would lessen as well. These lies trapped me in fear. I couldn't talk to anyone about these things. Honestly, I wouldn't have believed it myself if I hadn't experienced it.

Here's the thing: If you are living with deception, how do you know that you are being deceived? The Bible calls the devil the father of lies. In heaven, Lucifer was called the light-bringer, son of the morning. In my own words, he had the best seat in the house, yet he wanted to rise above God and rebelled. God cast him out of heaven, and one third of the angels followed him. Lucifer passionately hates everything that God loves. According to Genesis 1:27, we were created in the image of God; therefore, Satan hates God's most precious creation: you and me.[37]

The devil is known as a thief. Scripture says, "A thief has only one thing in mind – he wants to steal, slaughter, and destroy. But I have come to give you everything in abundance, more than you expect – life in its fullness until you overflow!"[38] The devil is counterfeit to everything God is. God is the Father of love, truth and all things good. The devil is the father of lies, hate, and all things evil. Wait a minute, the devil is a father?

As Jesus was talking to the Pharisees, He said, "You are the offspring of your father, the devil, and you serve your father very well, passionately carrying out his desires. He's been a murderer right from the start! He never stood with the One who is the true Prince, for he's full of nothing but lies

---

[37] Isaiah 14; Revelation 12
[38] John 10:10 TPT

– lying is his native tongue. He is a master
of deception and the father of lies!"[39]

Thoughts to Ponder

Before we go any further, consider your view of God.
What do you know about Him? What do you believe
about Him? Do your thoughts and beliefs align with the
Bible? Or like me, do you have some conflicting beliefs?
Our experiences form our opinions and beliefs. When
those experiences are repeated; they are reinforced. The
more something is reinforced it becomes truth to our
souls even if it is a lie. What we think, know, or believe
about God rules our entire lives. It is how we see the
world, and how we act and react with others. If we
believe God to be critical and judgmental, then we may
be critical and judgmental of others. If we believe God to
be merciful, then we may be willing to extend mercy to
others as well. We act out what we believe whether that
is good or bad.

---

[39] *John 8:44 TPT*

THE TRUTH REVEALED
CHAPTER 9

From Father to Papa
Throughout the years, God has shown me over and over His love towards me. When I'm hurting, I don't run from Him anymore but rather straight into His arms. When I was a little girl, I loved to play rough. For example, while trying a new trick on my bike, I would inevitably get hurt by falling and skinning my knee or scraping an elbow. When that happened, I would run screaming to my mom. I knew that if I could get to her, she would make the hurt go away. She would clean me up and put a Band-Aid on my booboo. I expected her to kiss the bandaged area every time. Somehow, that kiss made the pain not hurt as much.

My dad, however, had another perspective entirely. He and I liked to wrestle and rough house. In my childhood home, we had a large dining room in the middle of the house. There was plenty of room to run circles around the table. My dad and I would chase each other around that table quite often. He would laugh, and I would scream and giggle as I ran. Sometimes He would reverse and try to catch me the other way. It was so much fun; I cherish these memories. Nevertheless, without fail, I would trip. I'd lose my balance and run into the wall, hit my head, or fall and get carpet burn on my knee or elbow. I would cry, and my dad would laugh advising me that I should shake it off. He would remind me that I was tougher than that, but I wanted sympathy. The phrase, "rub some dirt in it, you'll be fine" comes to mind. My dad knew I wasn't really hurt, and I was laying it on thick for extra attention.

But I remember when my dad taught my sister to ride her bike without training wheels. She was going so fast that he was running as hard as he could to catch up to her. Boom! She crashed head on into a stop sign at full speed. I remember my dad's face turned white as a sheet as he nestled her gently against his chest. He carried her the entire way home. I watched the love that he displayed when there was genuine pain.

God takes our wounds seriously. He desires for us to run to Him, and allow Him to carry us home. As we truly learn the heart of God, we will learn that He is completely trustworthy. His love for us is complete. It lacks nothing. If we allow Him, He will heal every single fear, hurt, struggle, pain, and disappointment we have ever experienced.

What we focus on is what we give power to in our lives. My focus slowly turned from Satan to Jesus and from the demonic to the angelic. When we realize that God is not embarrassed or surprised by our failures, we will feel the freedom to just be ourselves. Our eyes will be opened to His love and our hearts capable of receiving His comfort and wisdom as He counsels us through our shortcomings. There may be people in our lives who are embarrassed or ashamed of us, but God never is. People may turn their backs on us, but God never will. I love how Graham Cooke says it:

> "Even in the consequences of our action, the love of God reaches out to cover, protect, and nurture us in our wounded-ness. The biggest thing we get to learn is that God loves me for me! Not for what I can do. God's love helps us to relax about ourselves. The grace of God is given to us to enable us to feel loved when we mess up. God's grace enables us to feel good about God and, therefore, to have mercy on ourselves and others. We are a work in progress. No one condemns the artist of an unfinished picture. Instead we look at what is there, and we picture what it could become. We

wonder, we imagine, and we are excited by the possibilities."[40]

Grace is not given to us so we can live however we want and not worry about consequences. Grace is a gift given to us to empower us to walk in complete freedom from anything that would entangle us in bondage. Grace isn't a license to sin while flippantly abusing the sacrifice of the cross. Grace helps us overcome sin.

Lavished By Papa's Love

Every person on this planet has failed at one time or another. It doesn't matter how big or small; we have all failed. It's when we try to change ourselves in our own effort that we feel defeated. We also feel defeated when we strive to live up to other people's standards and expectations of us. It is only through relationship with Jesus and time in His presence that lasting change comes.

A number of years ago, I felt a strong "urge" to go to Arizona and attend a Mini Internship Bootcamp through Patricia King Ministries. This was a weeklong opportunity to get training in personal development, character, kingdom values, and so much more. It is one of the rare times when I have felt driven to be somewhere.

---

[40] *http://www.elijahlist.com/words/display_word_pf.html?ID=2207*

When I signed up for the bootcamp, I didn't even really know who Patricia King was. I just remember praying and asking God to allow me to see other believers who displayed Jesus' love and demonstrated His power. I wanted to see people in action who were walking, talking, and living like the church in the book of Acts. I had no idea my prayer was about to be answered. God showed me a healthy environment of a body of believers up close and personal who operated in the love, anointing, and power of the early church. Unbeknownst to me, I had a divine appointment with God; He was about to show Himself to me.

While in Arizona, I had so many first time, unique experiences. During lunch at Patricia King's house, I was talking to my new friend, Rhonda, when she asked one of the session speakers to join us. This man radiates the love of Jesus. My friend asked if he would pray over her to receive the anointing of love that God imparted to him. He gently laid one hand on her to pray and put his other hand on my head. As he prayed over us, where his thumb touched the crown of my head, I had a supernatural experience.

I felt a physical manifestation of love. I literally felt love! I couldn't see it with my eyes, but I felt it just like you can feel the wind caressing your face on a windy day. It felt like warm honey dripping down from the crown of my head. Slowly, this liquid sensation rolled down the back of my head, neck, and back. It was thick and warm, yet smooth.

In my heart I heard the words, "liquid love." I had never heard that phrase before, but I felt the warmth of Jesus' love pour over me. For the record, this liquid wasn't something that you could see with your eyes, but it was so real! It was a radical, amazing experience. The prayer he prayed was simple and quiet, yet the power that came out of his hand was a beautiful expression of who Jesus is. If I had been a 1970's hippie, I would have said, "Far out, dude!"

God is love. He doesn't only give love; He IS love. I was learning that love is everything with God. Oh, how I have struggled secretly with love my entire life! We can't love other people when we don't even like ourselves, much less love ourselves. We cannot give what we do not possess. As we allow God to heal our hearts, He increases our capacity to receive His love. As our hearts fill with His love, we find that it is so much easier to love ourselves and others.

TRUSTING THE SHEPHERD
CHAPTER 10

Psalm 23 is the most well-known psalm in the Bible. It's probably as famous as John 3:16! When things are too familiar, it's easy to gloss over the words and not really absorb the meaning. One evening as I was watching a movie, the phrase "read Psalm 23" kept intruding in my mind as if it were tapping me on the shoulder. I finally gave in, recognizing that the Lord must want me to read it. While I had memorized it a long time ago, I felt like I should actually open the Bible and read the words. I asked God to give me a fresh perspective and to help me see what it was He wanted to show me.

> The Lord is my best friend and my shepherd. I always have more than enough. He offers a resting place for me in his luxurious love. His tracks take me to an oasis of peace, the quiet brook of bliss. That's where he restores and revives my life. He opens before me pathways to God's pleasure and leads me along in his footsteps of righteousness so that I can bring honor to his name.

Lord, even when your path takes me through the valley of deepest darkness, fear will never conquer me, for you already have! You remain close to me and lead me through it all the way. Your authority is my strength and my peace. The comfort of your love takes away my fear. I'll never be lonely, for you are near.

You become my delicious feast even when my enemies dare to fight. You anoint me with the fragrance of your Holy Spirit, you give me all I can drink of you until my heart overflows. So why would I fear the future? For your goodness and love pursue me all the days of my life. Then afterward, when my life is through, I'll return to your glorious presence to be forever with you![41]

As I was pondering Psalm 23's meaning, I had a vision. I saw myself in a beautiful meadow with long flowing, deep green grass. Just a few meters from where I was, I saw a wide, gorgeous stream. There was a man standing there. Instinctively, I knew that this man represented the Father. I was a little nervous as I walked up to Him. He didn't say anything, but we began to walk together along the water's edge. I began to feel peaceful as I learned to relax. A few days later, I was reading Psalm 23 again. As

---

[41] Psalm 23:1-6 TPT

I thought about the vision by the stream, I went back into the vision. Except this time, I put my hand in the Father's hand as we walked together beside the stream. Walking hand in hand, He was taking me to another level of trust and healing towards how I felt about Him and how I viewed Him. I was beginning to feel safe and secure in His presence.

Is there a longing in your soul to walk quietly hand in hand with God beside the still waters? Is your heart crying to feel His peace and to know His presence? God loves you passionately. He is constantly pursuing a relationship with you. He longs to restore your view of Him, so you can walk with Him and talk with Him just as Adam and Eve did.

God will speak to you in a very personal and unique way. If you desire these kinds of experiences, God will give them to you. He is no respecter of persons,[42] but He is a respecter of faith.[43] God speaks personally to us in a way that we can understand. He can speak in dreams, visions, the Bible, a conversation, nature, movies, music, or the arts. There is no limit to the methods He will use to speak to us. We just need to believe that He wants to speak to us, and then believe that it's really Him when He does!

---

[42] Acts 10:34
[43] Hebrews 11:6

A Shepherd I Can Trust

If we don't have an accurate view of who the Father is, then it's next to impossible to gain complete healing. Why? Because if we don't have trust in the Shepherd, we will not follow where He is leading. I can't tell you how many times I didn't like where He was leading me; therefore, I made my own way. Choosing my own direction caused me trouble 100% of the time. #badidea #godswayisbetter #shepherdknowsbest

Trust in the Lord completely, and do not rely on your own opinions. With all your heart rely on him to guide you, and he will lead you in every decision you make. Become intimate with him in whatever you do, and he will lead you wherever you go. Don't think for a moment that you know it all.[44]

As our hearts begin to believe that God is good, we are able to trust Him. That's why God took so much time showing me that He was good. I had numerous experiences that deceived me into thinking He was not very good. However, I've come to understand that following His path and His way leads me to more than enough of anything I have needed in my life.

---

[44] Proverbs 3:5-6 TPT

As we see in Psalm 23, God offers a resting place in His luxurious love. Love is our Shepherd. His path leads us to true rest in His heart. How many times have you just wished that your soul would be at rest? God promises to restore our souls. How? Through emotional healing! Complete trust isn't easy, but God is good! He is leading us down our best path! And as we learn to trust Him, our perspective shifts to see His goodness in everything. When things look dark, there is a certain trust that brings an unexplainable peace. When hard things come, we don't fear.

After my daughter left home, I was depressed and functioned on autopilot for the first three years. She and I had shouting matches. I said things I regret. I pushed too hard and held on too tight. I was a wounded soul trying to help another wounded soul.

Sometimes our circumstances will back us into a corner, and we have to choose. Will we surrender everything and trust God, or will we continue to choose our own understanding? While worry certainly tormented me, there was something inside me that knew trusting God was the only way out. Things got ugly quite a few times. Kayla made some bad decisions, and my husband and I were dealing with her choices. Two of her "friends" threatened her life and ours. Other family members were in crisis as well. At the same time, I was dealing with my own shame, rejection, and other soul issues. Plus, my relationship with my husband was strained due to all the stress. To make matters even worse at that time, the church we were attending shut its doors.

I mean it when I say that we need to learn to trust God in every single situation. Trust me; I've had lots and lots **and lots** of practice to choose to trust Him or not. I've learned that trusting God is always the best choice because He never fails!

But trusting God doesn't mean that He meets our every expectation. He often jumps outside the box that we've put Him in. He'll do things differently, or the results will not be what we had hoped. In all transparency, I got aggravated with God. It took time to build the level of trust He asks for and deserves. Nevertheless, trust is beautiful when you grasp it. Love and trust are intertwined.

During my daughter's senior year of high school, the Lord told me that Satan was going to try to take Kayla's life. I remembered my own horrific senior year, and I asked God how to pray for her protection. I daily prayed Psalm 91 over her, plead the blood of Jesus over her, and released angels of protection around her.

On a holiday weekend that year, one of her friends was bringing her back to our home when their vehicle flipped and landed upside down in the ditch. My husband and I were at my sister's house. When my sister's phone rang, we ignored it because we didn't recognize the number. The answering machine came on, and we heard this frantic voice shrieking from the machine. My sister was like, "who is that?" Immediately, I knew it was Kayla! A mother knows. By the grace of God, Kayla and her friend walked away with only a few cuts and bruises. It was a true miracle. God answers prayer!

Trusting God is a continual choice. Sometimes, I have questioned things that have happened that did not feel like He was a good God. Some situations do not feel like they are in our best interest, but ultimately, they are bringing us closer to our destinies. I don't have all the answers; regardless, still I choose to trust.

Maybe you have had a loved one pass through eternity's gates even though you were trusting God for healing. My heart hurts for you. It's hard to trust when we don't understand the outcome. My own dad died less than a year ago unexpectedly and tragically. Pain is real. Things happen in life that flat-out suck! Nevertheless, I have chosen to trust God in every circumstance even though it hurts like hell. I may get angry, but He understands. He loves us. He is there to comfort us. No matter what happens, God is good. He is not the author of suffering. Rather, there is an evil devil that comes to steal, kill, and destroy our lives.

Butterflies

One day I asked God why I have had such a long and painful path. He started talking to me about butterflies. When a butterfly is in a cocoon, it is alone. There is a lot of activity inside that cocoon. A metamorphosis is taking place. Once the internal work is done, the butterfly struggles until it bursts through the cocoon. Then, what used to be an ugly caterpillar now emerges as a beautiful butterfly.

Science advises that if one were to help the struggling butterfly to emerge from the cocoon, it would die. The struggle is what makes the butterfly strong and able to survive. God put me in a cocoon to heal my heart and transform my mind. By the time I broke out of the cocoon, He had completely transformed me. I now have the confidence and the permission to *"Simply BeYOUTiful!."* And you will too!

RELIGION VERSUS JESUS
CHAPTER 11

Searching for Truth

Church hurt is real. Toxic Christians exist. For example, one church asked me to leave instead of offering counsel or a path to restoration. Looking back, the church probably was not equipped to handle my depth of pain, but at the time, all I felt was another rejection. Then, three other churches that I invested in closed their doors. The pain of these events was real. As God revealed His true character to me, He also showed me the difference between a religious Christian culture and true, intimate relationship with Jesus. It is in the religious Christian culture where toxic Christian behaviors are developed.

Is God pleased with our Western church culture? Christians are supposed to be the Body of Christ. We are commanded to love one another, be united, and stay connected. While we attend services in buildings and call it church, it's really not. We, the people, are the church. Unfortunately, the church is better known for being condemning, judgmental, and critical. Where is the love that we are supposed to be known for? Jesus said, "By this everyone will know that you are my disciples, if you love one another," (John 13:35 NIV). If people are running from the church and not towards it, we have to ask why. It's not okay to maintain religious traditions simply because, "It's how my great-granddaddy done it, and we ain't changin' it." That's my Southern version.

Have you ever looked at a dollar bill? Have you ever wondered whether it was real or counterfeit? Do you know how federal agents are able to detect if a bill is counterfeit? They spend time looking at the real thing. When we have experienced what God's love really is, we are able to detect when love isn't being demonstrated. For example, in the church, we force behavior modification through fear, shame, and intimidation. "Love will never invoke fear. Perfect love expels fear, particularly the fear of punishment. The one who fears punishment has not been completed through love," (1 John 4:18 Voice). Jesus gives us free will and never forces His love one anyone.

On the opposite spectrum, there is another kind of love where everyone is comfortable. There is no internal change or freedom. This love tells you only what you want to hear. The messages are diluted, and sin is never addressed. This leaves everybody broken and deceived.

God once told me in prayer, "There is a power in love that brings willing change." Jesus walked in this love, this power, because everyone He met was impacted. Change was inevitable for those who encountered Jesus – except for the Pharisees. The Pharisees were more concerned about proving Jesus wrong and discrediting Him than caring if people's lives were changed. #theoriginaltoxicchristians

Jesus challenged the Pharisaical traditions. He challenged their way of thinking. He challenged the way they interacted with people. Jesus exposed them for who they really were: bullies who took advantage of those under them. The sad thing is that this attitude is prevalent in our current church culture. Don't be deceived! The Pharisees are alive and well.

Pharisees

Who were the Pharisees? They were the Jewish religious leaders. They followed the Law of Moses, but they also added to it. There were a number of Rabbinic laws; these were laws created by the Rabbis. In many cases, the Rabbinic laws (or man-made laws) were created to benefit the Rabbis who created them. (Sad, but true.) When Jesus came, He followed all the Law of Moses; however, He refused to allow the Pharisees to put their man-made rules on Him. The Pharisees were known to care more about their Rabbinic rules and religious traditions than they did about the commandments handed down from Moses. Basically, many Pharisees lived as if their traditions were more important than God's laws.

Traditions made the Pharisees appear to be obeying God. I call the modern day Pharisee's Toxic Christians. Let's look at an example in scripture. I have emphasized the word tradition in the text.

> You disregard and give up and ask to depart from you the commandment of God and cling to the **tradition** of men [keeping it carefully and faithfully].
>
> Thus you are nullifying and making void and of no effect [the authority of] the Word of God through your **tradition**, which you [in turn] hand on. And many things of this kind you are doing.[45]

The Pharisees were more concerned with the rules handed down by the elders of the past than they were with the actual commandments that God gave to Moses. These men cared about rules more than they did people.

---

[45] Mark 7: 8, 13AMPC

Do you see any similarities between them and the church today?

One time I witnessed a woman being sternly corrected because of what she wore to church. What if that had been her first time there? What if she didn't have any other clothes? Another time, a woman was crying because she was having a genuine touch from God. Instead of allowing the Holy Spirit to minister to her, she was asked to leave the sanctuary. Why? The leaders felt she was being too loud and was distracting others. I can picture Jesus sitting with this woman outside the church as they both wept. The traditions and service outline was of upmost importance in this church just as it was in the temple with the Pharisees. What if we need someone to be real and raw in our worship services? What if allowing her to wail would have shifted the atmosphere for everyone else to receive a touch of God's love too?

Isn't the church supposed to be a hospital where the wounded come to get healed? Instead, we have created an atmosphere of perfection. We don't have ushers; we have bouncers. Anyone who doesn't look the part, or who might disrupt the status quo isn't allowed past the veil. Jesus wouldn't be allowed in many of our church services.

Religious Mindset

If you take the time to read Matthew, Mark, Luke, and John you will see that Jesus had more conflict with the religious folk than anyone else. I find that interesting. Most of the organized church in that day rejected Jesus. Jesus was constantly violating the Pharisees' rules. He confronted these religious leaders who were abusing the people through their legalism.

According to the dictionary, legalism in theology is: "The doctrine that salvation is gained through good works. The judging of conduct in terms of adherence to precise laws."[46] In other words, legalistic people are those who try to look holy on the outside with no connection to God's Spirit. These people have a tendency to find it difficult to show love. The only time Jesus got angry was when He confronted the religious leaders. If you read the entire chapter of Matthew 23, you will see for yourself what Jesus thought of the Pharisees.

What's tragic is that the Pharisees knew the prophecies of the coming Messiah, yet missed Him when He came. They did not receive what God was doing in the earth through Jesus. He wasn't the Messiah they expected, so they rejected Him. The Pharisees denied the very

---

[46] https://www.dictionary.com/browse/legalism

salvation for which they were waiting and watching. Remember, the Pharisees were the religious leaders of the day. Jesus warned His disciples, "Make sure you are not influenced by the hypocrisy and phoniness of the religious leaders. It permeates everything they do and teach, **for they are merely serving their own interests**," (emphasis mine).[47] Oh, that we as a church would not become so prideful that we miss what God wants to do in this hour!

Religion says I know all about God, but I don't really want to know God. This was me for most of my life. I had a lot of head knowledge, but not a lot of experience with who God really is. There were too many negative experiences mixed in with half-truths from the Bible. I think there are a lot of Christians who are religious and have an honest desire to pursue God, but simply don't know how. Ironically, it is their very religion that hinders their relationship.

That's why God took the time to show me who He really is. I couldn't gain any kind of lasting or deep healing if I didn't know the character of God. Intimacy with God is imperative. If we read our morning devotion without conversing with God, where is the intimacy? A

---

[47] Luke 12:1 TPT

conversation is two people talking. In order to have a conversation with God, we need to give Him a chance to speak back to us. Too often we do our religious duty by reading the Bible or our devotional book, but we stop just short of relationship. The enemy has fooled us into believing that we are being good Christians because we check something off our list. Can I be honest? Jesus would rather we take 10 minutes to sit quietly and listen for His voice than read the Bible for 30 minutes. #mysheephearmyvoice

When I was a teenager, I was completely in love with Rocky Balboa (Sylvester Stallone). Rocky was my hero; Rocky III was my favorite movie. I was so obsessed with the movie that I recorded the movie on cassette tape! (Remember those?) I would listen to it while getting a tan in my backyard. I had the movie memorized. I could even do a pretty good Mr. T imitation. I watched the movie repeatedly. I was surprised my parents didn't throw the VHS away!

I read all kinds of things about Sylvester Stallone. Did I know him? No, I knew some personal facts because I read about him, but I didn't know him personally. Heartbreaking for my teenage self, I never got to hang out with him or have a conversation with him. I used to pray that Sylvester Stallone would get saved. #forreal #notkidding #rockyrules #teenagerinlove

Here's the thing: Religion tells us that we must attend all the church functions to draw near to God. Whatever you do, don't discuss the fact that so much activity leaves you exhausted and not enough time with your family. You'll be "marked" rebellious and unfaithful to God. Seriously? If we really think about it, does it even make logical sense? Honestly, this used to intimidate me until I'd finally had enough. Healthy boundaries are important. Jesus doesn't put pressure on us. Whenever you're feeling pressure, it's a good place to pause and ask God why.

> As Jesus and the disciples continued on their journey, they came to a village where a woman welcomed Jesus into her home. Her name was Martha and she had a sister named Mary. Mary sat down attentively before the Master, absorbing every revelation he shared. 40 But Martha became exasperated by finishing the numerous household chores in preparation for her guests, so she interrupted Jesus and said, "Lord, don't you think it's unfair that my sister left me to do all the work by myself? You should tell her to get up and help me."

The Lord answered her, "Martha, my beloved Martha. Why are you upset and troubled, pulled away by all these many distractions? Are they really that important? Mary has discovered the one thing most important by choosing to sit at my feet. She is undistracted, and I won't take this privilege from her."[48]

Every time I read that passage, the movie Indiana Jones and the Last Crusade comes to mind. During one scene, Indiana Jones enters the room where an old knight is protecting the Holy Grail. The bad guy follows Indiana into the room. The room is filled with many different cups, but only one is the Holy Grail. The bad guy asks the knight which cup is the Holy Grail. The knight says, "You must choose. But choose wisely! For as the true grail will bring you life, the false one will take it from you."[49] The bad guy grabs the most beautiful cup assuming that it is the Holy Grail. Thinking that he will obtain immortality, he drinks from the cup. The man almost immediately dies, and the old knight looks at Indiana and says, "He chose poorly." Indiana begins to look more closely at all the cups in the room. Finally, he chooses the most

---

[48] Luke 10:38-41 TPT
[49] https://www.youtube.com/watch?v=A0TalLrtZ24

humble cup and drinks. The knight says, "You have chosen wisely."[50]

To Jesus: Martha chose poorly; Mary chose wisely. Intimacy trumps service every time. We are to serve, but with a heart full of love. Our actions or service were never meant to be out of obligation or a way to earn our way into heaven. "For it was only through this wonderful grace that we believed in him. Nothing we did could ever earn this salvation, for it was the gracious gift from God that brought us to Christ! So no one will ever be able to boast, for salvation is never a reward for good works or human striving."[51]

Orphan Mindset

Inside each of us is a desire to be loved and accepted. A person with an orphan mindset believes that they are not worthy and do not deserve to be loved. This mindset says you have to work or earn love to be accepted. It's someone who feels like he is on the outside looking in without a sense of belonging.

This used to be me. I didn't always have an orphan mindset. It developed over time because of the rejection

---

[50] https://www.youtube.com/watch?v=A0TalLrtZ24
[51] Ephesians 2:8-9 TPT

I felt. In order to protect myself, I made vows of self-protection. For example, I said, "I'll never trust the church again. I'll never allow someone to make me feel that way again. I'll never express how I truly feel or give my opinion because it just causes pain." I was worried that I would be rejected because somehow my performance wouldn't measure up, or I would be viewed as stupid. This is an example of an orphan mindset.

Thankfully, there is hope! The apostle Paul in his letter tells us, "The Spirit you received does not make you slaves, so that you live in fear again; rather, the Spirit you received brought about your adoption to sonship. And by him we cry, "Abba, Father."[52] God's love helps us to overcome the orphan mindset. I can now serve people out of love because I know I am a daughter of the King. I know my identity; I am secure in who I am. I serve Him out of the abundance of His love for me, not to gain His love and approval. Before we came forth from our mothers' wombs, He was watching over us. All of heaven rejoiced at our births. When we realize that we are valued, loved, and cherished, our perspective shifts. We view life and our problems through new lenses. We are then able to live life with a new confidence.

---

[52] Romans 8:15 NIV

One more thing: some people get comfortable in their place of pain. Their issues bring them attention and identity. They have developed a victim mentality. A victim is constantly listing all the bad things that have happened to them which is always someone else's fault. The attitude behind all their words is, "Woe is me; everything bad always happens to me."

Things happen to all of us that are not within our control; however, that does not negate our need to take responsibility for our lives and our decisions. This is a crucial element to moving forward in our healing journey. We work through the painful portions of our lives; we don't choose to stay there. When God heals our hearts, it is vital that we choose to move from the place of pain. We have to stop looking in the rear view mirror, and focus our vision on what's in front of us. Remember, God reveals to heal. He does not condemn us, but rather seeks to help us. #nocondemnation #youcandoit #babysteps

BREAKING THE RELIGIOUS MINDSET
CHAPTER 12

To give you a better understanding of my journey, we talked about the religious mindset and the Pharisees. When Kayla walked out, God sent two friends who helped me through some of my darkest days. One day one of those friends looked at me and said, "Shannon, you have a religious spirit." DOH! Talk about a punch in the gut! The statement literally took my breath away for a few seconds. Holy cow! He told me that I was struggling with the very thing I hated in others. OUCH!!!

Even though my feelings were hurt by my friend's statement, it didn't send me further into depression. Why not? This person genuinely cared for me. We were friends, and my heart knew he was speaking from a heart of love. I wanted truth – even if it was going to hurt – as long as it came from a heart of love with good intentions. I didn't need any more shame or judgment.

The first step to freedom is recognizing the lie that has held us captive in any area. I had a religious spirit, and I didn't even know it. This spirit just about ruined my life

– literally. The weight of obligation, the religious spirit, legalism, and tradition have pushed countless people away from the arms of Jesus, the church, and sometimes, even their own families.

Eyes to See

I had a vision once where Jesus came and washed my eyes. This washing enabled me to see clearer into the spirit realm. The truth is that I cannot help others obtain freedom if I am imprisoned by my own issues. I cannot lead others where I, myself, am unwilling to go.

> "Why would you focus on the flaw in someone else's life and yet fail to notice the glaring flaws of your own? How could you say to your friend, 'Let me show you where you're wrong,' when you're guilty of even more? You're being hypercritical and a hypocrite! First acknowledge your own 'blind spots' and deal with them, and then you'll be capable of dealing with the 'blind spot' of your friend."[53]

I used to believe that authenticity was the enemy. I believed that anytime I was transparent it was used as a weapon against me. It was as if I handed someone a

---

[53] Matthew 7:3-5 TPT

loaded gun, and then ran around with a target on my back. I believed if I wore a mask, people couldn't see the real me. If they can't see me, then they can't hurt me. The enemy entangles us in so many lies! I developed an ungodly belief of unworthiness. I believed that if something was wrong, it was my fault. I believed that I had ruined my entire life; there was no hope for the future. It was unredeemable. And since nothing I did was ever good enough, why try?

I lived my life stumbling through the thick fog that the combination of my experiences, religious spirit, and orphan spirit had created around me. I was stuck on a roller coaster ride of seeking God for relief only to end up in the same place of misery. My emotions controlled me; after awhile, I enjoyed my pity parties. That's not God's fault. He continuously reached out to me. I just couldn't see Him clearly through the fog. I would gripe and complain about all the people who hurt me. But when Jesus washed my eyes, it was like the clouds began to give way. I could finally see.

While I loved God, the church hurt was real. We stopped attending a local church for awhile after I was asked to leave a church as a young adult. It took me a long time to have the courage to step foot in a church again. God is so faithful! My husband and I decided to start visiting a

Pentecostal church that I had attended many years prior. The pastor asked me to come forward during the service. I was so hungry for relief from my pain that I agreed. He knew nothing about what had happened in my past. My heart was pounding so loudly that it sounded like a set of drums! I begged God not to embarrass or "expose" me. I didn't want any more pain.

The pastor said that he saw me sitting in a prison cell. He said that God didn't put me in the prison but that I had put myself in the cell. The prison door was wide open, but I was afraid to come out. I was sitting there because I believed I deserved to be there. The pastor then asked if God could take my hand and walk with me out of that cell, into freedom. As a prophetic act, I took the pastor's hand. We walked back and forth together for a few minutes. It felt weird at first; nevertheless, as we walked, I felt a weight lift off me. I could see Jesus holding my hand, walking me out of the cell. By the time we were done, I was ugly crying! The relief was incredibly intense; the crushing pressure on my chest was gone!

Though that experience was years ago, it is forever etched in my heart. There was no guilt, no shame. It was a beautiful experience of a body of believers coming together to pray and uplift someone in pain. This was a healthy church experience.

When we repent of our sins, God remembers our sins no more. While there are natural consequences to our actions, the guilt has been removed. It's the religious mindset that wants to keep us bound, not God. It reminds us of what we have done and holds us in shame. The devil is the accuser; unfortunately, he influences people with the religious mindset to never let us forget our mistakes and regrets. The Bible tells us, "Your hand-to-hand combat is not with human beings, but with the highest principalities and authorities operating in rebellion under the heavenly realms. For they are a powerful class of demon-gods and evil spirits that hold this dark world in bondage."[54]

Hearing God's Voice

While you've read about some of the experiences I have had with God, keep in mind that these happened after spending time waiting for Him to speak to me. Remember, I have been in church my entire life. I prayed and read my Bible (sometimes); however, it was more of ritual to check off my religious list. Sometimes I would feel His presence, but the real shift came when my heart changed. When I believed that He loved me and was worthy of my trust, that's when I began to experience

---

[54] Ephesians 6:12 TPT

Him. There are still days when I hear Him more clearly than others, but I know He is speaking.

Do you remember the dial radios? You had to turn the knob back and forth to find the clearest frequency. If the dial was just a little too far to the right or the left, you would only hear static or distorted words. As you fine-tuned the dial, the sound became clear. That's how it is listening to God; some days we have our spiritual radios more finely tuned than others.

How do you hear from God? I can only speak from my experiences. God uses just about everything to illuminate a truth: the Bible, movies, music, nature, and every day experiences to name a few. At first, I learned to hear Him through journaling and praying. By praying, I mean talking and taking time to listen. I gave Him a chance to speak, and I didn't control the entire conversation by speaking about all of my needs and then walk away. That's not relationship. Sometimes I would ask Him a question, and wait for His response. As you learn the sound of His voice, it gets easier and easier.

Just like anything else, learning to hear God takes practice and time. But know this: God will NEVER say anything that contradicts His word (the Bible) and His character. I would confirm everything with the Bible.

This helps to guard our hearts and keep us from being deceived. Think of praying as talking to a friend. Both people take turns talking and listening to each other. Prayer is the same way.

One time when I was learning to understand when God was speaking to me, I was jamming to some tunes in my car. All of a sudden, a particular person's name popped in my head. I thought to myself, "I haven't thought of that person in a long time. Where did that come from?" Remembering that I was becoming more aware of God's voice, I asked Him if He was speaking. I felt like He said yes, so I prayed for the person. After about a minute, I felt like I should call her. When she answered the phone, I asked how she was doing. She explained that it was hard day, but my phone call meant the world to her! I felt a prompting to call her. I didn't hear an audible voice from Heaven saying, "Call So-in-So." Hearing God is learning to respond to the random thoughts that pop into our heads, and by faith move forward with them. This is another example of the church in action. Simple and simply beautiful!

Intimacy with Jesus

I now have a real, authentic relationship with Jesus. He consistently pours out His love and His heart. He gives me unforgettable experiences with Him. Oh, how He longs to have that time with you as well! Jesus has a specially designated spot in His heart for you. No one else can fill it. When we don't take the time to have relationship with Him, I believe that portion of His heart stays empty.

Jesus set me free from having head knowledge about Him to having encounters with Him. The experiences I had with Him were amazing. Some were downright fun. He laughed with me. He cried with me. When I needed comfort, I pictured Jesus wrapping His arms around me. This is intimacy with the One who created us. He wants relationship. It's been said that intimacy means "Into-me-see." I allowed Jesus to see my heart. He already had, but now I was a willing participant.

Jesus' love is so powerful and strong. That's what the gospel is all about: the love of God. That's why they call it good news! If you had cancer in your body and Jesus healed you, wouldn't you say that's good news? If you were starving for something to eat and Jesus brought you a big, fat juicy burger with a tall order of fries, wouldn't you call that good news? If you were tormented night after night with panic attacks and Jesus came to bring you peace, wouldn't you call that good news? If you were staring at a list of all your past mistakes and regrets and

Jesus ripped up the list telling you that you are forgiven, wouldn't you call that good news? The good news of the gospel is that we are loved, forgiven, and adopted as children of God.

We are representatives of Jesus on earth. He gave us all authority when He went to heaven. We are the ones who put our arms around a lonely person. We are the ones who lay hands on the sick, and they recover. We are the ones who cast out demons. We are the ones who feed the hungry. We become the hands and the feet of Jesus. We go in His name and in the power of His love. It's beautiful!

As we grow in relationship with Jesus, we find that it is easier to surrender every area of our lives to Him. When we give Him access, He awakens us to the reality of His kingdom in our everyday lives. The apostle Paul put it this way, "My old identity has been co-crucified with Messiah and no longer lives; for the nails of his cross-crucified me with him. And now the essence of this new life is no longer mine, for the Anointed One lives his life through me—we live in union as one! My new life is empowered by the faith of the Son of God who loves me so much that he gave himself for me, and dispenses his life into mine!"[55]

---

[55] Galatians 2:20 TPT

TOXIC SHAME
CHAPTER 13

The Woman at the Well
God helped me understand His true character. He really is a good God. I was no longer afraid of Him. He showed me the difference between religion and relationship. Even though I had made great strides in my journey, my heart was still clothed in shame. Now that I trusted God, He was able to approach the subject. It may sound odd, but I have always felt a level of shame simply for being female. Why? Because of the way our society and Christian culture treat women. Did Jesus respond to women in the same manner? Take a moment and ask Jesus to give you a fresh perspective as you read John 4:5-30 from the Passion Translation.

> Jesus arrived at the Samaritan village of Sychar, near the field that Jacob had given to his son, Joseph, long ago. Wearied by his long journey, he sat on the edge of Jacob's well. He sent his disciples into the village to buy food, for it was already afternoon.

Soon a Samaritan woman came to draw water. Jesus said to her, **"Give me a drink of water."**

Surprised, she said, "Why would a Jewish man ask a Samaritan woman for a drink of water?"

Jesus replied, **"If you only knew who I am and the gift that God wants to give you—you'd ask me for a drink, and I would give to you living water."**

The woman replied, "But sir, you don't even have a bucket and this well is very deep. So where do you find this 'living water'? Do you really think that you are greater than our ancestor Jacob who dug this well and drank from it himself, along with his children and livestock?"

Jesus answered, **"If you drink from Jacob's well you'll be thirsty again and again, but if anyone drinks the living water I give them, they will never thirst again and will be forever satisfied! For when you drink the water I give you it becomes a gushing fountain of the Holy Spirit, springing up and flooding you with endless life!"**

The woman replied, "Let me drink that water so I'll never be thirsty again and won't have to come back here to draw water."

Jesus said, **"Go get your husband and bring him back here."**

"But I'm not married," the woman answered.

"That's true," Jesus said, **"for you've been married five times and now you're living with a man who is not your husband. You have told the truth."**

The woman said, "You must be a prophet! So tell me this: Why do our fathers worship God here on this nearby mountain, but your people teach that Jerusalem is the place where we must worship. Which is right?"

Jesus responded, **"Believe me, dear woman, the time has come when you won't worship the Father on a mountain nor in Jerusalem, but in your heart. Your people don't really know the One they worship. We Jews worship out of our experience, for it's from the Jews that salvation is made available.**

From here on, worshiping the Father will not be a matter of the right place but with the right heart. For God is a Spirit, and he longs to have sincere worshipers who worship and adore him in the realm of the Spirit and in truth."

The woman said, "This is all so confusing, but I do know that the Anointed One is coming—the true Messiah. And when he comes, he will tell us everything we need to know."

Jesus said to her, **"You don't have to wait any longer, the Anointed One is here speaking with you—I am the One you're looking for."**

At that moment the disciples returned and were stunned to see Jesus speaking with the Samaritan woman. Yet none of them dared to ask him why or what they were discussing. All at once, the woman dropped her water jar and ran off to her village and told everyone, "Come and meet a man at the well who told me everything I've ever done! He could be the Anointed One we've been waiting for." Hearing this, the people came streaming out of the village to go see Jesus.

The woman at the well was shunned, an outcast in society, and full of shame in the midst of her sin. We see the heart of Jesus as He broke religious and traditional taboos. History shows that the Samaritans were considered half-breeds; the Jews hated them. Racism existed even then, and the fire of animosity between the two groups raged. Jewish men did not talk to Samaritan women – for any reason, period!

This woman, rejected by society, a complete outcast, and full of shame, had a real encounter with Jesus. She went to the well at the hottest part of the day to avoid dealing with people. She knew that everyone whispered about her. She was aware of her past. She wanted to draw the water and return to her hut of safety. But the Father had another plan! Jesus met her at the well. He let her know that she was not invisible. He saw her! Jesus speaks truth to her tenderly and full of wisdom. He intentionally initiates a conversation, going against the societal norm. But Jesus doesn't care about the laws or the traditions of man. He is more concerned about showing love.

There was a time in my life when I was this woman. I was the loose woman, with twisted morals, and a wounded heart, rejected and scorned within Christian culture. The Jesus that met the woman at the well was not the Jesus that was portrayed to me when I was confronted or ignored. Because of this, shame became my constant companion.

What is shame? According to Merriam-Webster, shame is defined as, "a painful emotion caused by consciousness of guilt, shortcoming, or impropriety."[56] Shame is bad, but it can get worse! When shame goes beyond an emotion, it becomes toxic. This happens when it's not simply a feeling; it's your identity. You haven't made a mistake; you are the mistake.

We've all felt shame on some level. Maybe you were embarrassed and wished you could sink right through the floor. Maybe your kids said something in the grocery store or to their teacher that you can't believe popped out of their mouth. Maybe you farted during a business meeting. Come on now, it's real life! I know you're laughing at that example. It's always funny when it's someone else.

However, toxic shame is no laughing matter. When does shame become toxic? Shame has the ability to turn toxic when we are treated harshly or constantly corrected. It can easily turn toxic if we have been physically, emotionally, or sexually abused. With repeated shameful

---

[56] *https://www.merriam-webster.com/dictionary/shame*

behavior, regardless of personal choice, our hearts are unable to separate what is happening to us from who we are. Toxic shame calls us unworthy. Shame doesn't become toxic overnight. It happens over time, like a small bucket sitting under a leaky faucet. If left unattended, the leak fills the bucket to overflowing. When our shame reaches that point, it has reached the point of toxicity.

Jesus' View on the Samaritan Woman

Never once did Jesus use shame as a tool for correction. Remember, Jesus initiates the conversation, which completely shocks the woman at the well. Jesus, a Jewish man, acknowledged a woman who was a Samaritan. This chick is one tough cookie to me. She is sassy, full of spunk, and she puts up a fight. It's as if she is covering her pain as though it doesn't bother her. Nevertheless, Jesus responds to her every question in an intentional, noncombatant manner. He is gracious and engaging. He offers her a drink of living water, so that she will never thirst again. If she drank what Jesus offered, she would be forever satisfied.

This woman previously had five husbands and was now living with her boyfriend. Jesus didn't ignore the facts about her life; He acknowledged them. For someone to have had that many husbands and now a live-in boyfriend, she was obviously thirsty for something in her life. There was something in her soul that needed to be satisfied. The woman sought to quench her soul's thirst and find her identity from men.

Finally, she recognized Jesus as the promised Messiah. Here is the man she had been looking for all her life! Here is the man that could satisfy the depths of her soul! Immediately, shame lost its grip, and she ran into the very village where she was considered an outcast.

Consider the magnitude of what happened: a Samaritan woman was proclaiming that the Jewish Messiah was this man named Jesus. She loudly and openly shared her story to the very people who had whispered about her and avoided her in the first place. That's freedom! No longer hiding due to fear and shame, one conversation with Jesus made her soul whole. Can you imagine the radiance on her face as her shame was removed?

Guess what? The people actually listened to what she had to say. They listened and responded to this outcast. They believed the good news of Jesus. That's what preaching is supposed to be, by the way, telling the good news about Jesus. All she did was share her personal story of how she came face to face with Jesus. He satisfied every longing in her soul. No more shame. No more guilt. No more hiding. #freedom #fearless

STRAIGHT UP STUPID
CHAPTER 14

I remember being given a timed math test in first grade. When we were finished, the teacher asked us to individually come to her desk so that she could grade our work. My little heart was racing because I did not remember what I had learned. While trying to complete the quiz, my mind went blank.

When I walked up to the desk, the teacher looked at my paper. Eternity passed; then, with a bright, red pen, she scribbled a big fat zero across the entire page and threw it across the room without a word. As I started to tremble, every eye was on me. Holding back the tears, I picked up my paper and scurried to my desk. Traumatized, I put my head down on the desk covering my face with my arms. I believed that as long as no one saw my face, I would be okay even though I heard the snickers from my classmates. Shame found an open door in my heart that day.

When I was in third or fourth grade, I overheard my Papaw yelling at my Mamaw in the kitchen one day that

I was S-L-O-W while they were trying to help me study. He was all up in her face screaming like it was her fault. I was horrified that my Mamaw was getting in trouble because I was stupid. Oh the shame I felt! Throughout the years I've heard so many phrases about my intelligence; therefore, I used to freeze every time I had to take a test or speak in public, for fear of appearing stupid.

In high school, I was elected student government treasurer. The student officials were sworn in at an all-school assembly. When the student body president called me to the stage, I quietly asked him to give me a few words to repeat at a time. Unfortunately, he didn't hear me (or ignored me). He started rattling off words so fast that I only repeated the few words I could remember. I started moving my lips not allowing any sound to come out so that it looked like I was repeating after him. Truth be told, he sounded like Charlie Brown's teacher, "Wahwah Wahah Wa." The good news was that I remembered my name; the bad news was that one of the teachers almost fell out of her chair, laughing so hard. While it's hilarious now; back then, it was catastrophic. While I laughed it off, it was one more experience that further confirmed the lie that I had believed.

One day I had a random thought to look up the meaning of my name. Jesus was speaking again! The name

Shannon means "wisdom, wise one" or one translation says "possessor of wisdom." So, every time someone says my name, they are actually calling me "wise one or possessor of wisdom." Isn't that hilarious? Jesus has such a sense of humor. Jesus knows each one of us and planned our lives out before the foundation of the world.

When my parents named me, God was already working against the lies that would attack my life. He knew the things that would come against me, and He already had a solution prepared. When I got a job, I worked in bookkeeping for 12 years. Despite my belief that I wasn't good at math, I was very successful. God can redeem everything! Take that, devil!

Toxic Shame & Inner Torment

Shame of any kind makes us want to hide. At first, we want to cover what we did, but when it becomes toxic, we strive to conceal who we are. Church should be a place where we go to heal. Unfortunately, too many of us have found the church to be a place of judgment – even more harshly if you struggle with any type of sexual sin. To make matters worse, some Christians like to share our personal confessions as prayer requests, retelling our stories without skipping details.

My dad wasn't aware of the sexual trauma I had experienced. I was scared. I didn't want him to end up in jail because he had to go kill somebody. He probably would have too. My mind went crazy with all kinds of scenarios. I felt I needed to protect my parents from my pain and shame. I determined that it was better to suffer in silence rather than to see anyone else hurt. Plus, "forgive and get over it" was ingrained in my brain.

We can forgive someone, but the emotional trauma still needs healing. These wounds are the perfect breeding ground for the devil to create more chaos in our lives. Here's the thing: trauma opens the door for inner torment. Merriam-Webster defines torment as, "1: extreme pain or anguish of body or mind : agony; 2: a source of vexation or pain."[57] It is pain so deep that words cannot accurately explain it.

Inner torment is complete torture. In order to gain release, many people inflict harm to their bodies. People do different things out of self-loathing and torment. Some are obvious while others are not – like cutting. Personally, I gained a lot of weight and became a closet smoker on and off for years. I escaped in romance novels and binged on movies.

---

[57] https://www.merriam-webster.com/dictionary/torment

We rehearse in our minds the trauma we've experienced as well as our own shortcomings. It's like we're running on a hamster wheel of memories, and we can't figure out how to get off. The memories keep replaying because we need healing. However, the only way to get healing is to talk about it. If we discuss what really happened to us, we fear further rejection and trauma. Therefore, we keep everything inside, hidden, and out of sight. We portray a happy-go-lucky person on the outside, while the shame and torment are slowly killing us inside.

How Jesus Handles Sexual Shame
Jesus treats people much better than the religious leaders and Christian Culture. There was a woman who was caught in the act of adultery as recorded in John eight. The religious scholars dragged her to the temple where Jesus was teaching and made her stand exposed in front of everyone. Can you imagine the shame she was experiencing? The arrogance of these men amazes me as they used this woman in an attempt to trap Jesus.

> Then they said to Jesus, "Teacher, we caught this woman in the very act of adultery. Doesn't Moses' law command us to stone to death a woman like this? Tell us, what do you say we should do with her?"

They were only testing Jesus because they hoped to trap him with his own words and accuse *him of breaking the laws of Moses.*

But Jesus didn't answer them. Instead he simply bent down and wrote in the dust with his finger. Angry, they kept insisting that he answer their question, so Jesus stood up and looked at them and said, **"Let's have the man who has never had a sinful desire throw the first stone at her."** And then he bent over again and wrote some more words in the dust.

Upon hearing that, her accusers slowly left the crowd one at a time, beginning with the oldest to the youngest, with a convicted conscience. Until finally, Jesus was left alone with the woman still standing there in front of him. So he stood back up and said to her, **"Dear woman, where are your accusers? Is there no one here to condemn you?"**

Looking around, she replied, "I see no one, Lord."

Jesus said, **"Then I certainly don't condemn you either. Go, and from now on, be free from a life of sin."**[58]

Where was the man who was in bed with her? Why didn't they bring him to stand before Jesus as well? Was it because he was someone the religious leaders knew? Is it because society always places the blame on women? When you think about it, HOW did these men know what was going on at that time with those two people? The Law of Moses states that BOTH the man and the woman were to be stoned for sexual sin.

In the passage above, we see that Jesus took the attention off of the woman. Instead of pointing fingers, Jesus wrote in the dirt. What He wrote may always remain a mystery; nevertheless, it caused the men to cease their accusations. Every single man lowered his stone and walked away. Jesus then asked the woman where her accusers were.

Jesus handled the situation with grace and dignity. He treated the woman with love and respect. When she looked in the eyes of Love, her entire life changed. While the Law dictated death, Jesus extended forgiveness and

---

[58]John 8:4-11 TPT

gave her permission to be free. Jesus demonstrated grace and mercy toward the woman caught in adultery.

In today's Christian Culture, grace has been abused. One viewpoint says, "Live however you want, there's grace." On the opposite spectrum, another viewpoint says, "People will never learn their lesson and change if we give them grace." True, authentic grace gives us the strength, desire, and ability to change. The question is: do we want to change? Do we want to look into the eyes of Love and receive His forgiveness and be rid of our shame?

IT'S A WONDERFUL LIFE
CHAPTER 15

God speaks to me so much through movies! I absolutely love getting sucked into a good story. I love how God uses different ways to speak to us. One Christmas, I was watching my all time favorite Christmas movie, "*It's a Wonderful Life.*" It's about a man named George Bailey who felt that his life had been full of trials. George was bitter because he gave up his dreams and desires to stay home and take over the family business. He felt pressure to always do what was right and needed. At his all-time low, he wished he had never been born. An angel came down and granted George his wish. George saw how horrible the town was without him. Everyone he loved had difficult lives without joy. When he was able to recognize how many lives he had impacted for the better, he realized he had a wonderful life.

When George was 12, he saved his brother, Harry, when he fell into a frozen river. When Harry went to war, he shot down 15 planes. Two of those planes were attacking a troop transport. Harry received the Medal of Honor. If

George had not saved Harry, he wouldn't have been around to save countless lives in the war.

When George was a boy, he worked for a pharmacist delivering medication. When George's boss, Mr. Gower, had learned his son died in the war he was filled with grief. He wasn't paying attention and accidentally filled a prescription with poison. George kept him from going to prison by not delivering the medicine. George was able to help a lot of people get homes and live better lives. In the movie, George was given a beautiful gift to see what life would have looked like without him.[1]

As I was watching, *It's A Wonderful Life*, Papa God whispered so clearly, "Shannon, I don't make mistakes." He reminded me that my life was important. He planned my life. He chose my gender with a beautiful plan in mind. Papa God also told me I would not fully know the lives that I have impacted for the better until heaven. At the end of the movie, I heard Him whisper again, "Will you allow Me to show you your life through My eyes and change your perspective?" A change in perspective is vital to seeing our life through God's eyes. I know deep in my heart that I have made a difference in other people's lives in a positive way. Guess what? So have you!

Heavenly Encounter with Jesus

As I was spending time with the Lord, I felt like He gave me a heavenly encounter. This was not an open vision like when you look around your house and see your couch. The pictures were in my mind's eye, but I was fully awake. The images were very clear. It wasn't spooky or weird, but as natural as remembering a dream after resting. This was the first time this had ever happened!

As I sat before the Lord and focused my mind on Him, I saw myself lying face-up in the middle of a beautiful, blue room in a white robe with a blue, silk ribbon. Suddenly, Jesus walked into the room. He walked up to me; His eyes full of love made contact with mine. He washed my hair, eyes, and hands. Then, Jesus touched my mouth. He never spoke a word, but the way He looked at me overflowed my heart with love and acceptance. Peace saturated my entire being.

When my encounter was over, I asked Jesus to explain what had happened. I wanted scripture to test what I experienced. Jesus told me that He washed my hair to signify the cleansing of my mind from negative beliefs and lies.[59] He washed my eyes so that I could see Him clearly.[60] Jesus washed my hands to purify me from my

---

[59] Ephesians 5:26; Psalm 51
[60] Revelation 3:18

personal sins.[61] He added that my hands were now anointed to do the work He assigned. He touched my mouth to represent the forgiveness of generational sins and iniquity.[62]

I have never felt the love of Jesus consume me like this before! After it was over, I was awed because I felt like I didn't deserve it with all of the anger and bitterness that had been inside my heart – especially towards God. Yet, Jesus loved on me. All I did was set aside quiet time to focus on Jesus; He met me right where I was. I had my eyes closed and focused on His goodness as best I could. It was an act of faith. I wasn't scared or ashamed. His unconditional love made me feel safe.

As I have spent more time with Jesus with a healthy perspective of His character, a whole new world has opened up to me. I am able to see and hear Him much more clearly. I've come to recognize that when I am at rest and relaxed, I hear God more clearly. When we strive to hear God, it is more likely that we won't hear anything. Peace and stillness attract the Spirit of God. The Lord tells us to "Be still and know that He is God."[63]

---

[61] Psalm 24
[62] Isaiah 6:6-8
[63] Psalm 46:10

My heart in sharing my vision is to let you know that Jesus wants to wash you too! Whatever shame you've held, whatever pain holds you captive, Jesus wants to cleanse you and give you the ability to experience His love and freedom! Jesus is the same for everyone. He wants you to experience Him in a very real, tangible, and personal way.

If you want to experience God, just let Him know. You can pray something like this: *"Lord, I know that You are good. I know that You are not a respecter of persons. I know that what You do for one of Your children, You can do for me too. I want to know You in a new way. Will You help me to hear Your voice? Will You show me visions? Will You give me expressions of Your great love for me? And when You do, help me to recognize that You are speaking to me. In Jesus name."*

FEAR

CHAPTER 16

What is fear? The dictionary defines fear as, "1a: an unpleasant often strong emotion caused by anticipation or awareness of danger; b (1) : an instance of this emotion; (2) : a state marked by this emotion."[64] But wait! There's more! Fear can also be defined as "profound reverence and awe especially toward God." [65] It can be difficult to understand that there are two kinds of fear: healthy and unhealthy. Healthy fear warns us of danger. In relation to God, healthy fear reminds us how small we are and how big God is. Unhealthy fear builds roadblocks to progress; it becomes a paralyzing force that keeps us bound.

God is the creator of all things good. Satan, on the other hand, has no creative abilities at all. He is a master of deception and the father of lies![66] He is a thief, and his ultimate goal is to steal, kill, and destroy in any way he

---

[64] https://www.merriam-webster.com/dictionary/fear
[65] https://www.merriam-webster.com/dictionary/fear
[66] John 8:44

can.[67] Therefore, Satan takes what is good and distorts it. Through his lies and deception, he destroys emotions, health, relationships, families, churches, cities, and the list goes on and on.

Fear affects all of our lives. Its chief aim is to hold us captive to lies that stop us from moving forward. What do you fear? What holds you back from pursuing your dreams and desires? Is it a fear of what people will think? Is it the fear of getting hurt again? Is it fear of failure? Is it fear of embarrassment? Is it fear of exposure? Or, is it the exact opposite: the fear of success? Many of us have a belief that God doesn't love us; therefore, we are afraid to approach Him. We fear intimacy with God because we view Him as an angry Father or a harsh taskmaster. These images of God stir up fear in our hearts, and we run from Him instead of to Him.

Fear ruled my world. I had a fear of rejection, separation, and abandonment. I feared shame and humiliation the most! I would often freeze in the middle of a conversation; I mean I would stop mid-sentence! My mind would go completely blank. I couldn't think. Unfortunately, this just added to my humiliation. People would just look at me like I was alien from outer space.

---

[67] John 10:10

Do you see the vicious cycle that Satan wants us trapped in? We live in a constant state of anxiety, avoiding relationships, and living in isolation. When we are so focused on fear, we stay trapped in that cycle. Fear keeps us from relationship, the very thing for which we were created.

"After Earth"

The movie, *After Earth,* is about, "A crash landing [that] leaves Kitai Raige (Jaden Smith) and his legendary father Cypher (Will Smith) stranded on Earth, 1,000 years after cataclysmic events forced humanity's escape. With Cypher injured, Kitai must embark on a treacherous journey to signal for help. They must learn to work together and trust each other if they want any chance of returning home."[68] The movie is well-known for Cypher's quote: "Fear is not real. The only place that fear can exist is in our thoughts of the future. It is a product of our imagination causing us to fear things that do not at present and may not ever exist. That is near insanity, Kitai. Do not misunderstand me, danger is very real, but fear is a choice. We are all telling ourselves a story, and that day mine changed."[69]

---

[68] http://www.sonypictures.com/movies/afterearth/
[69] http://www.imdb.com/title/tt1815862/quotes

I know that the movie quote says fear isn't real; however, we know that fear is very real. Throughout this movie, there were many examples of the different fears we face. God used the movie to help me understand that the emotional wounds tormenting me would get worse unless I faced these fears head on.

As I watched this movie, my heart swelled as I saw the example of a father and son reconciling their relationship. Through difficult circumstances they were forced to humble themselves and talk it out. In adversity, they focused on what was truly important: their relationship. No longer able to ignore each other, they faced their fears: their broken relationship, a scary beast, personal pain, and the loss of a loved one. In real life, we ignore our emotional pain because we are fearful of rejection resulting from vulnerability. What story is fear telling you? You have a choice to accept it as fact or fiction.

People Pleasing

Do you know any people pleasers? They often strive to keep peace, avoid conflict, and will almost always say yes. People pleasers are overwhelmed with obligations and living up to other people's expectations of them. One of their greatest fears is disappointing someone. Many believe that if they don't please others, they are a failure. On the other hand, if they choose to maintain healthy boundaries and say "no", people pleasers feel like they are being selfish. People pleasers keep their own thoughts and desires deeply hidden in their hearts. They always do what someone else wants them to do. Does this sound like you? I know it used to be me. It took a long time, but I finally became fed up with all of the obligations and expectations others placed upon me. I call them my "shoulds."

For the majority of my life, I had allowed people to dictate how I should think, feel, and act. I didn't allow myself to express my own value system and perspectives; I didn't have my own sense of self worth. I never took the time to evaluate my own personal principles, values, or morals when I became an adult. It wasn't until a few years ago that I could see the "shoulds" in my life masked my own fear and guilt for not meeting other people's expectations. I wasn't able to believe the truth about God because I didn't know what that truth was. All I knew was the *religious* God.

The "shoulds" in my life taught me how to be a perfect performer. I overemphasized my decisions based on what other people would think. I also put pressure on myself to "get it together" without dealing with what caused me to feel this way. Relationships tend to be extremely superficial when we are people pleasers. When we have the freedom to be our authentic self instead of looking and acting like a carbon copy of someone else, relationships become healthy, deep, and meaningful.

There is a vast difference between doing something for someone out of love and constantly trying to please someone. A person who does something out of love has healthy boundaries and is secure in their own identity. The people pleasing person has poor boundaries. They are often unsure of their identity because they sacrifice it on the altar of fulfilling everyone else's needs. Without even knowing it, everyone else's need becomes an idol in their lives.

If you take the time to think about it, the more we try to please someone, the more demanding they become. They never seem to be satisfied with what is offered. We seek their respect and validation, which has the opposite effect. Instead, the controlling person loses respect for the people pleaser. Pleasing our heavenly Father is the true desire of our hearts, but this happens through relationship. It is not striving to maintain a set of dos and don'ts. This one hit home for me. Sometimes, when we think we are being selfless, we are being disobedient to God.

Speaking from experience, learning to set and maintain boundaries is difficult. It's even harder if the people with whom we are setting boundaries is used to getting their own way in our lives. Nevertheless, if we continue to allow God to heal our identity, their tactics won't intimidate us any longer. My identity was attacked through criticizing, demeaning, judging, withdrawing emotionally (the silent treatment), shaming, and yelling. People also used scripture to try to make me feel guilty for setting a boundary. People pleasing and poor boundaries are connected to the spirit of fear.

"Jungle 2 Jungle"

In Disney's movie, *Jungle 2 Jungle*, "Michael Cromwell (Tim Allen),is a self-absorbed, successful commodities broker, living in New York City. Wanting to marry his new fiancé, Charlotte, he needs to obtain a final divorce from his first wife, Patricia, who left him years earlier. Patricia now lives with a semi-westernized tribe in Venezuela. Michael travels there to get her signature on divorce papers, but, upon arriving, discovers he has a 13 year old son, Mimi-Siku."[70] When they finally meet, Michael feels obligated to take his son back to New York and get to know him.

Back in New York, Michael tries to resume his life as normal. He needs to go to the office although his son wants to spend time with him. Michael wants to pretend that the knowledge that he has a son hasn't changed his life. However, the truth is that having his son in New York with him changes everything. Michael tells his son that he is obligated to go to the office.

Never hearing the word obligated before, Mimi-Siku asks his dad what that word means. Michaels says, 'when you do something that you don't really want to do.' Later on, Michael gets frustrated because his son wants to go see the Statue of Liberty, but he is too busy. He tells his son that he has a life here and that everything can't change just because he showed up.

Hurt, Mimi-Suki asks his dad why he even brought him to New York in the first place; Michael says that he feels obligated. Mimi-Suki is devastated. He remembers what obligated means and says, "You're obligated to be with me?" Then Mimi-Siku runs away, crushed to learn that he

---

[70] https://www.imdb.com/title/tt0119432/plotsummary

is an obligation. After this, Michael chooses to spend time with his son developing a deep love for him.

In the end, Michael doesn't want to live without his son and is willing to change his life in order to have a relationship with him. Michael's perspective changed when he viewed his son through a new set of eyes. The knowledge that he had a son and the interruption of his narcissistic life was the best thing that could have happened to him. This movie illustrates someone who shifted from obligation and "shoulds" to a relationship of love.

THE TRUTH REVEALED
CHAPTER 17

W
e will no longer fear what other people think once the truth about our own identity and worth is revealed. God gives us people who compliment our own uniqueness while encouraging us to become our best. They celebrate us and not simply tolerate us.

God is the creator of all things good. Nothing He created is bad, nothing. We said earlier that God created fear. Our natural emotions of fear are fight, flight, or freeze. I like to say the only difference between fight and flight is the letter "L". The "L" is to pause and shout, "Lord, help!"

For example, when my sister and I were little, we had a big playhouse in the backyard. The neighborhood kids always came over to play. One day, I walked into the playhouse to find a girl had cornered my sister. She was hitting my sister! I froze. My mind was still trying to process that my sister was in the corner crouching, down with her hands over her head crying. Once I got over the shock, my second response was straight up fear. I ran, and I kept running. In my defense, the girl was two years older and bigger. But then it hit me! I had abandoned my sister in the playhouse with no help. Yep, just left her there!

You know how dramatic kids are in the first place, and I kept thinking I'm a bad sister. I was really freaking out and trying to think what to do next. Finally, I ran into the garage and grabbed a baseball bat and ran screaming like a banshee into the playhouse. I was swinging the bat around, half-crazy with fear, screaming for her to get off of my sister. When it was over, I was shaking so bad I didn't think I'd ever stop. My sister ended up not really being hurt, and the girl went home. In the awesome ways of children, everyone became friends again not long after that. However, the girl never did bully my sister again.

Imagine a bug falling in your hair. What do you do? You begin to do the war dance, shaking your head like crazy while your hands are trying to keep up with your head to brush the bug off – all the while screaming at the top of your lungs. Meanwhile, everyone else is trying not to fall on the floor because they're laughing so hard. Been there, done that!

Healthy fear makes us courageous enough to stand up against the class bully. Healthy, natural fear keeps us from walking up to a wild lion thinking we can get him to purr. What do we do when we encounter a wild beast in the woods or on a nature trail? Freeze, process the situation, and then back away very slowly to safety. These are powerful survival reactions. God did not give us a spirit of fear, but He gave us the Holy Spirit who gives us His mighty power, love, and self-control. When we think of fear as only a negative emotion, we want to avoid it. Reverential fear is created for worship. "Let all the earth fear *and* worship the LORD; Let all the inhabitants of the world stand in awe of Him."[71]

The glory of the Lord fills us with a holy fear. We are filled with such awe that all we can do is cry out in worship. When we have a healthy fear of the Lord, the fear of man falls away. The Psalmist declared, "Now I know, Lord, that you are for me, and I will never fear what man can do to me.[72] So we can say with great confidence: 'I know the Lord is for me and I will never be afraid of what people may do to me!'"[73]

Before the apostle Paul wrote a majority of the New Testament, he was known as Saul of Tarsus. He was a Pharisee who was full of anger and wanted to kill the

---

[71] Psalm 33:8 AMP
[72] Psalm 118:6 TPT
[73] Hebrews 13:6 TPT

disciples of Jesus. He asked for a letter from the high priest for permission to arrest any man or woman who was a follower of Jesus in Damascus. The following is the biblical account of Saul's first encounter with the Lord.

> *So he obtained the authorization* and left for Damascus.
>
> Just outside the city, a brilliant light flashing from heaven suddenly exploded all around him. Falling to the ground, he heard a booming voice say to him, **"Saul, Saul, why are you persecuting me?"**
>
> The men accompanying Saul were stunned and speechless, for they heard a heavenly voice but could see no one.
>
> Saul replied, "Who are you, Lord?"
>
> **"I am Jesus, the Victorious, the one you are persecuting. Now, get up and go into the city, where you will be told what you are to do."**[74]

Saul encountered a holy fear of God that changed his life forever. Jesus changed his name from Saul to Paul. God used Paul to literally change the world, and his writings

---

[74] Acts 9:3-7 TPT

are still impacting us today. Paul faced persecution without fear knowing that God would take care of him.

Love Never Brings Fear

Love never brings fear, for fear is always related to punishment. But love's perfection drives the fear *of punishment far* from our hearts. Whoever walks constantly afraid of *punishment* has not reached love's perfection. Our love for others is *our grateful response* to the love God first demonstrated to us.

Anyone can say, "I love God," yet have hatred toward another believer. This makes him a phony, because if you don't love a brother or sister, whom you can see, how can you truly love God, whom you can't see? For he has given us this command: whoever loves God must also demonstrate love to others.[75]

Have you ever said, "I love God, but I hate people."? In anger, I've said those words, many times. Frustrated, I have said, "Ugh, I hate church people." We cannot love God if we can't love people. Through all of the wounds that we experience, God gives us a way to release the hurt

---

[75] 1 John 4:18-21 TPT

and gives us a choice to forgive. Love in its purest form is beautiful. When I had the vision of Jesus washing me, the peace and love that I experienced was nothing I have beheld before that time. Jesus saw everything that I had done as well as everything that had been done to me. He even knew all the judgmental words that I had ever spoken and all the judgmental words spoken against me. He washed it all. In that moment, I had never felt more beautiful.

God is worthy of our adoration! He is worthy of us standing in awe of His greatness and goodness. We can look around and see the splendor of who He is in all of nature, yet take it for granted. He is constant and faithful, never wavering in His love for us.

God's Splendor (Psalm 8)
Lord, your name is so great and powerful! People everywhere see your splendor. Your glorious majesty streams from the heavens, filling the earth with the fame of your name!

You have built a stronghold by the songs of babies. Strength rises up with the chorus of singing children. This kind of praise has the power to shut Satan's mouth. Childlike worship will silence the madness of those who oppose you.

Look at the splendor of your skies, your creative genius glowing in the heavens. When I gaze at your moon and your stars, mounted like jewels in their settings, I know you are the fascinating artist who fashioned it all!

But when I look up and see such wonder and workmanship above, I have to ask you this question: *Compared to all this cosmic glory*, why would you bother with puny, mortal man or be infatuated with Adam's sons?

Yet what honor you have given to men, created only a little lower than Elohim, crowned like kings and queens with glory and magnificence. You have delegated to them mastery over all you have made, making everything subservient to their authority, placing earth itself under the feet of your image-bearers.

All the created order and every living thing of the earth, sky, and sea— the wildest beasts and all the sea creatures everything is in submission *to Adam's sons*. Lord, your name is so great and powerful. People

everywhere see your majesty! What glory
streams from the heavens, filling the earth
with the fame of your name![76]

Whoa! No wonder the devil hates us so much and works
so hard to bring destruction in our lives and chaos to our
relationships. The fear of the Lord brings wisdom and
understanding. When we worship the Lord, it shuts the
devil down. I once heard that gratefulness and praise is
heaven's worship music while murmuring and
complaining is the music of hell.

When we are consistently complaining and critical, we
give the devil power to wreak havoc. If we would return
to our childlike wonder and behold the beauty of the
Lord, our perspective would shift from the fear of man to
a divine and healthy fear of the Lord. The wisdom and
knowledge that I received to allow the Lord to heal my
dry, thirsty soul is available for you as well! We are not
alone in our journey or in our need of the Father!

> The starting point for acquiring wisdom is
> to be consumed with awe as you worship
> Jehovah-God.

---

[76] Psalm 8:1-9 TPT

To receive the revelation of the Holy One, you must come to the one who has living-understanding.

Wisdom will extend your life, making every year more fruitful than the one before. So it is to your advantage to be wise. But to ignore the counsel of wisdom is to invite trouble into your life.[77]

Lifestyle of Love

What does a lifestyle of love look like? Is it even possible? Where is the love in the church? Our society has distorted and watered down the meaning of love. It has become a flimsy feeling that can change with the wind, but real love is constant and never changes. Love is a choice.

Love, the Motivation of Our Lives

If I were to speak with eloquence in earth's many languages, and in the heavenly tongues of angels, yet I didn't express myself with love, my words would be reduced to the hollow sound of nothing more than a clanging cymbal.

---

[77] Proverbs 9:10-12 TPT

And if I were to have *the gift of* prophecy with a profound understanding of God's hidden secrets, and if I possessed unending supernatural knowledge, and if I had the greatest gift of faith that could move mountains, but have never learned to love, then I am nothing.

And if I were to be so generous as to give away everything I owned to feed the poor, and to offer my body to be burned *as a martyr*, without the pure motive of love, I would gain nothing of value.

Love is *large and* incredibly patient. Love is gentle and consistently kind to all. It refuses to be jealous *when blessing comes to someone else.* Love does not brag about one's achievements nor inflate its own importance. Love does not traffic in shame and disrespect, nor selfishly seek its own honor. Love is not easily irritated or quick to take offense. Love joyfully celebrates honesty and finds no delight in what is wrong. Love is a safe place of shelter, for it never stops believing the best for others. Love never takes failure as defeat, for it never gives up.

Perfect Love

Love never stops loving. It extends beyond the gift of prophecy, which eventually fades away. It is more enduring than tongues, which will one day fall silent. Love remains long after *words of* knowledge are forgotten. Our present knowledge and our prophecies are but partial, but when love's perfection arrives, the partial will fade away. When I was a child, I spoke about childish matters, for I saw things like a child and reasoned like a child. But the day came when I matured, and I set aside my childish ways.

For now we see but a faint reflection of riddles and mysteries as though reflected in a mirror, but one day we will see face-to-face. My understanding is incomplete now, but one day I will understand everything, just as everything about me has been fully understood. Until then, there are three things that remain: faith, hope, and love—yet love surpasses them all. So above all else, let love be the beautiful prize for which you run.[78]

---

[78] 1 Corinthians 13:1-13 TPT

Let all of our words and deeds be motivated by love! God's love and the love we desire to portray to one another looks like 1 Corinthians 13. For God so loved the world He gave us His son, Jesus. Love is safe. Love is freedom. Love is light. Love is power. Love conquers shame. Love conquers fear. Love conquers darkness. Love conquers sickness. Love conquers depression. Love conquers the fear of man. Love conquers all. Love has a name: Jesus!

THE DEVIL'S GAME
CHAPTER 18

Bitterness

When we view our lives through the lens of toxic shame and fear of exposure, we actually delve deeper into darkness. The painful memories of words and deeds are consistently playing on the screen of our minds. Unforgiveness grows like a weed and becomes a bitter root deeply entrenched in our soul. Before we know it, despair is our constant companion. We spend our lives nursing our wounds because it is the only thing we can focus on. We believe that if we actually forgive those who have hurt us, then they will not be held accountable for their actions. We believe that there will be no consequences for them, and they will get off scot-free. We definitely can't forgive ourselves because we must be punished for our mistakes.

When we want to ease these powerful, destructive emotions, the opposite actually happens. These bitter roots cause us to set up emotional walls to protect us from vulnerability. We make vows to protect ourselves from being hurt. These vows keep us bound to our brokenness. For example, we might say, "I will never allow myself to be vulnerable again; or, no one will ever have the power to hurt me like that again." The truth is that these vows are a defense mechanism to avoid shame and judgment. Unfortunately, because we are unable to obtain relief from our inner turmoil, we do the very things that bring about shame and judgment in our lives. We believe the lie that there is no escape from this inner turmoil; thus driving us deeper and deeper into a pit of hopelessness.

This is the vicious cycle that brings a lot of joy in Satan's kingdom. The things that we think will bring us freedom and happiness actually take us further into a cycle of unforgiveness, toxic shame, and bitterness. When this happens, thinking about going to Jesus makes us want to run and hide. We cringe at the thought of Jesus shining His light on these dark places. We don't want Him to see these things – let alone us. The truth is He sees them, and still opens His arms wide to us.

War in the Mind

The war in our minds is real! Some days we feel as though we are caught in the middle of a tug-of-war game. It's as if there is an angel on one side of us and a demon on the other. Both are tugging us to bend our will for either good or bad. Have you ever felt like no matter how hard you try, the same experience happens over and over again? I know I have! Have you ever tried to make changes, yet the results remain the same? The truth is that unhealed wounds leave us in emotional trauma; this gives the devil permission to work against us and affect those around us.

I like to think of our mind as the connecting muscle between our spirit and body. What we think becomes what we believe. What we believe becomes our behavior. Therefore, our behavior is the result of what we think. It's a never-ending cycle until the circle is broken. Even though I changed my behavior, I didn't change my thought patterns. I was never able to achieve lasting freedom until I changed my thoughts. What we latch on to and believe in our thoughts will dictate our lives. What we think, what we really believe, and what we say out loud need to be in alignment and agreement. For decades, I rehearsed bad experiences in my mind. I believed the ugly things people said. I believed the lies that bombarded my thoughts. The lies I believed became like self-fulfilling prophecies continually manifesting in my life.

Shame & Blame: The Devil's Game

Our society likes to play the shame blame game. We love to share our opinions with or without the facts. We love to point fingers on Facebook, in politics, at work, at church, and at home. It's a deceptive game that makes us feel justified. We believe we have a right to our feelings; thus, we ignore any conviction of our actions. We proceed to issue judgments against anyone and everyone. We walk right into Satan's trap to keep us divided through unforgiveness.

"If a house is divided against itself, that house cannot stand."[79] This applies to our own hearts as well. When our hearts are divided, we open the door for more destruction in our lives. Have you ever seen a dog lick a wound? He nurses that wound continuously by licking it. They even make collar cones to go around a dog's neck to keep their mouth away from the wound, so it has time to heal. The same is true with our emotional wounds. We lick our wounds by playing them over and over in our minds. We keep the shame blame game going by pointing the finger at everyone else. It's not easy to be willing to look in the mirror and evaluate our own attitudes and actions. Pride is the root of the shame blame game. It's

---

[79] Mark 3:25 TPT

always someone else's fault. We do whatever we can to avoid taking any responsibility.

Bah-Humbug

Most people have seen a version of *A Christmas Carol* by Charles Dickens. My favorite stars George C. Scott who plays Ebenezer Scrooge. He was a grouchy, stingy, cold-hearted, bitter, old man that no one could stand. On Christmas Eve, three ghosts visited him.

The first ghost showed him his past. The ghost revealed a little boy who was wounded and rejected by his father. His mom had died in childbirth, and his dad blamed her death on Scrooge. His first boss loved him. He had the hope of a happy life, and the possibility of true love. But instead of taking what was offered, Scrooge buried himself in his work. He believed that money would make up for the pain that he felt. He believed he had to first earn a place in this world, then he would be worthy of love. Scrooge couldn't grasp that love was offered freely; he felt he needed to perform.

The second ghost showed Scrooge the present. He learned what people really thought about him. Scrooge also saw how his employee, Bob Cratchit, lived without material blessings. Scrooge also observed that Cratchit's family was full of love. Even though Scrooge treated Cratchit poorly, he watched his employee show him honor. Then the ghost took Scrooge to his nephew's house. Scrooge's sister was the only one that had truly loved Scrooge. When she died, Scrooge hardened his heart; he didn't want to feel pain. He couldn't handle being around his nephew because the nephew reminded him so much of his sister; therefore, Scrooge chose to ignore his nephew even though he desperately wanted a relationship with his uncle.

The third ghost showed him the future. He watched as Cratchit's family ate dinner with little Tiny Tim's seat empty. This sweet little boy died because Cratchit couldn't afford the surgery needed. The ghost then showed Scrooge his own grave. Scrooge saw that no one mourned him. The third ghost never spoke, but the powerful message needed no words. Scrooge saw how blind he had been. He had allowed his wounds to fester and cloud his judgment. He finally understood that his choices and decisions affected the lives around him.

When Scrooge awoke on Christmas morning, he was so relieved to be alive that he let go of all his pain, bitterness, and stinginess. He jumped on his bed. He ran around with glee. This bitter, grouchy man regained his childlike wonder of the world around him. When his eyes opened to the truth, he had a perspective shift. His actions changed because his heart had changed. And because his heart changed, he was able to have meaningful relationships. The story of Scrooge is an excellent illustration of transformation. The difference between the man who was in bondage to his pain and the man who was grateful and free is dramatic. While not everyone will be visited by three ghosts on Christmas Eve, we all have a choice: living by our past pain or living in our present reality. If we choose to let go and live in the moment, we will see better tomorrows.

Grace

The word grace is used a lot in the Bible and in Christian circles; yet, it can be a difficult concept to grasp. Check out this definition:

> "In Western Christian theology, grace has been defined, not as a created substance of any kind, but as 'the love and mercy given to us by God because God desires us to have it, not necessarily because of anything we have done to earn it', 'Grace is favour, the free and undeserved help that God gives us to respond to his call to become children of God, adoptive sons, partakers of the divine nature and of

eternal life' It is understood by Christians to be a spontaneous gift from God to people 'generous, free and totally unexpected and undeserved' – that takes the form of divine favor, love, clemency, and a share in the divine life of God."[80]

Our heart is a garden. It is our responsibility to tend it. We need to make sure the soil is good for growing and keep the weeds out. When hurtful things happen, they are like seeds planted in the soil of our hearts. We water them and empower them to grow by replaying the memories in our minds. The Bible says, "Watch over each other to make sure that no one misses the revelation of God's grace. And make sure no one lives with a root of bitterness sprouting within them which will only cause trouble and poison the hearts of many."[81] Without grace, a root of bitterness sprouts within us; not only does it poison us but also poisons the hearts of those around us.

In the story of Ebenezer Scrooge, he didn't receive grace from his father. He was barely acknowledged. He was sent off to a boarding school so his father wouldn't even have to look at him. Through this lack of grace, the wounds of his life festered, and he grew to become a

---

[80] https://en.wikipedia.org/wiki/Grace_in_Christianity#cite_note-1
[81] Hebrews 12:15 TPT

bitter, old man. Based on his father's treatment, it is no wonder that Scrooge believed he needed to earn people's love and trust.

Just as Scrooge's wounds affected everyone, so do ours. Our behavior affects other people whether we want to admit it or not. The first portion of Hebrews 12 talks about receiving correction from God just like a parent corrects their kids. Discipline from God is not punishment; God's discipline is validation of adoption into His family.

However, discipline and abuse are two different things. With our own kids, we don't want them to suffer. We correct them to protect them. Discipline is always for the purpose of restoration in relationships. But when correction is given without love, it only adds fertilizer to the wound. Thus, bitterness takes root in our souls. Anytime emotional, verbal, or physical abuse is present, grace is absent. God revealed the truth to me regarding how I was handled in certain situations. His revelation helped me to forgive and pull up the bitter roots in my heart.

When a leader or parent has unhealed pain, it often passes down to the person under their authority. This creates a toxic cycle. I have watched people disciplined through judgment, shame, and inflexibility. This has pushed these people further into darkness. A person disciplined through love and grace is reminded of their identity. They are reminded of who they are IN Christ. The power of grace reminds us of who we are and whose we are. Grace is not a license to sin.[82] Grace is more than God's unmerited favor;[83] Grace is the currency of heaven flowing down to us through Jesus to empower us to live out God's best.

Love and grace push us toward being the pure Bride of Christ. Romans chapters five and six discuss grace's triumph over sin. Grace enables us to see ourselves through Jesus' eyes; thus, making it easier to believe who we can be. It is our responsibility as the Church to help each other grasp this beautiful revelation of grace.

In my vision of Jesus washing me, it was His grace and love pouring over me that removed the reign of sin, wounds, and pain. This grace brought purity into my life. As He washed my eyes, He gave me eyes to see as He sees. Suddenly, I was able to see clearly, and everything changed. Where sin abounds, grace abounds much more. Grace is more powerful than sin.

---

[82] Titus 2:11-15
[83] Ephesians 1:2-10

Forgiveness

It has been said that when we refuse to forgive and let something go, it is like drinking poison and hoping the other person will die. Unforgiveness and bitterness are poisons that will torment us and make us physically ill. God understands that forgiveness keeps us healthy and is beneficial to us. Even scientists are discovering that letting go of deadly emotions is crucial not only to our mental health, but to our physical health.

Let's look at what Jesus says about forgiveness:

> Later Peter approached Jesus and said, "How many times do I have to forgive my fellow believer who keeps offending me? Seven times?"

> Jesus answered, **"Not seven times, Peter, but seventy times seven times! The lessons of forgiveness in heaven's kingdom realm can be illustrated like this:**

> **"There once was a king who had servants who had borrowed money from the royal treasury. He decided to settle accounts with each of them. As he began the process, it came to his attention that one of his servants owed him one billion dollars. So he**

summoned the servant before him and said to him, 'Pay me what you owe me.' When his servant was unable to repay his debt, the king ordered that he be sold as a slave along with his wife and children and every possession they owned as payment toward his debt. The servant threw himself facedown at his master's feet and begged for mercy. 'Please be patient with me. Just give me more time and I will repay you all that I owe.' Upon hearing his pleas, the king had compassion on his servant, and released him, and forgave his entire debt.

"No sooner had the servant left when he met one of his fellow servants, who owed him twenty thousand dollars He seized him by the throat and began to choke him, saying, 'You'd better pay me right now everything you owe me!' His fellow servant threw himself facedown at his feet and begged, 'Please be patient with me. If you'll just give me time, I will repay you all that is owed.' But the one who had his debt forgiven stubbornly refused to forgive what was owed him. He had his fellow servant thrown into prison and demanded he remain there until he repaid the debt in full.

"When his associates saw what was going on, they were outraged and went to the king and told him the whole story. The king said to him, 'You scoundrel! Is this the way you respond to my mercy? Because you begged me, I forgave you the massive debt that you owed me. Why didn't you show the same mercy to your fellow servant that I showed to you?' In a fury of anger, the king turned him over to the prison guards to be tortured until all his debt was repaid. In this same way, my heavenly Father will deal with any of you if you do not release forgiveness from your heart toward your fellow believer."[84]

When we don't forgive, we are handed over to the tormenters. Does this explain the tug-of-war going on in your mind? Do you feel tormented all the time with these emotions by rehearsing them repeatedly? Do you see how refusing to forgive not only tortures our minds, but it affects our bodies as well?

---

[84] Matthew 18:21-35 TPT

From my understanding, long-term emotional toxicity plays a huge role in many cancer patients, and the stress of bitterness breaks down the immune system. Research it. We are taught that we should forgive those who have hurt us. When we experience pain, it hurts our soul with wounds that cannot be seen.

When we are physically hurt, we can locate the injury to determine how to treat it. If we break our arm, we understand that we have to wear a cast until the arm heals. When we choose to forgive someone by an act of our will, we give it to God and that takes care of the spiritual matter. Most people stop here. I know I did because I didn't know there was more. It felt incomplete, but I thought it was because I wasn't sincere enough. Even though we make the choice to forgive, there could still be wounds in our soul (mind, will, and emotions). When you think of someone who has hurt you, do all of the ugly feelings pop up? You may torment yourself with thoughts like, "I chose to forgive them, but why are all these negative thoughts and feelings still there?" If so, it's because your soul is still injured.

I think one of the toughest things I had to do was forgive myself for the choice to have an abortion my senior year. Yes, there was pressure from others, but ultimately the decision was mine. Oh, the emotional pain is indescribable! The torment of taking an innocent life is truly a nightmare. I have often wondered if the pastor I consulted would have counseled me instead of brushing me off would I have made a different decision.

Some Christians would say that I deserved every bit of torment that I felt. Nevertheless, Jesus opened His arms wide and led me to a place of healing. First, I repented. Then, I asked Jesus to tell my precious baby that I was sorry for making the wrong choice. I invited Jesus into the emotional trauma to begin the healing process. In my mind, Jesus and I journeyed back to my high school days. Together, we relived moments of trauma, and Jesus revealed to me that He was with me every minute. It took a long time to forgive myself as well as to forgive the cruelty of others during that time. When my inner healing had finally taken place, I felt both Jesus and my unborn baby's forgiveness in a tangible way. It's hard to explain, but I have the expectation and belief that my firstborn and Jesus will be waiting on me when I get to heaven. That's brings me peace and a beautiful hope.

It takes humility to forgive, but the peace that follows is almost tangible. There is a lightness that comes when we take a deep breath. Oh how I love the visual of old Ebenezer Scrooge; he sheltered himself from the pain of others and walled himself off so he would never feel pain again. Only it backfired, and he was never able to feel love or joy either. But when he let go of the need to protect himself from the pain, he was able to redeem what was left of his life. Ebenezer's latter days were better than his former days. We have this promise too! When we don't take our lives for granted, there is a richness that is added to each day. When we see the transformation of bitter to sweet in someone else's life, it brings hope for our own personal situations.

IT'S OKAY TO GRIEVE
CHAPTER 19

I t's okay to grieve. Grief is a natural emotion that comes with experiencing loss of any kind. Did you know that there are two types of grief? Healthy and Unhealthy. "Healthy grieving results in an ability to remember the importance of our loss—but with a newfound sense of peace, rather than searing pain."[85] When we choose to hold onto unforgiveness, we are experiencing an unhealthy grief. This grief is never-ending. If the wounds do not heal, the sorrow won't end. This grief screams, "Look at me! I'm suffering. No one knows what I am going through. No one knows the pain I feel. I suffer more than anyone else." Unhealthy grief also places blame on others. For example, people blame God when bad things happen. Some people will give God the silent treatment when someone they love was taken from their lives. This unhealthy grief is magnified and feeds off of the negativity of their thoughts and unhealed soul wounds.

---

[85] http://www.washington.edu/counseling/resources-for-students/healthy-grieving/

What causes grief? The death of a loved one. Suffering. An unfortunate outcome. Repeated bad behaviors. Unmanifested dreams. Job loss, etc. Even healthy grief can be difficult. Grief affects our spirit, soul, and body. Everyone moves through grief differently, and the methods used to overcome it will vary from person to person. In the natural process, we go through denial and withdraw wanting to be in isolation. We get angry and experience levels of depression. Healthy grieving ultimately leads us to a place of acceptance, and we are able to move forward, adjusting to the absence of what was lost. King Solomon wrote, "To everything there is a season, and a time for every matter or purpose under heaven...a time to weep and a time to laugh, a time to mourn and a time to dance."[86]

While writing this book, my dad died tragically and unexpectedly. He was a healthy 70-year-old man who was struck by a commercial truck while crossing the street. We were never even able to see his body. My dad and I were very close; I loved him very much. We walked together two mornings a week, and yes, he could out walk me. Ha! We were so much alike! We had great conversations and talked through hurtful situations from my early years. He didn't know about everything I went

---

[86] Ecclesiastes 3:1,4 AMPC

through, but he knew some.

Oh, how I miss him! Yet, I know that his legacy continues. He was a great man, and many, many people feel his lack of presence on this earth. To be honest, I was angry with God about how my dad was taken from us. Nevertheless, because God had already been healing my heart, I didn't stay in that place of anger. I was able to move forward, and you will too! It's okay to feel sorrow, anger, and pain. The key is to not allow bitterness to take root, but to allow the love of God into that place. Bitter roots entangle the good seeds in our hearts, thus robbing us of our future.

If we stay in the place of sorrow, ultimately, the pain will destroy us and our relationships. Ebenezer Scrooge played the shame blame game. Pride kept him from taking responsibility for his reactions to life's happenings. The ghosts forced him to look into the mirror of his own heart and his own mind. They didn't do it to be cruel. They did it because his life still had potential for great impact.

When my daughter left, it was like a final blow from the devil to bring destruction to my family. I love the phrase, "but God." There is always a "but God," when we earnestly seek Him. I had lived in a state of unhealthy grief for years, but God showed me the truth of what oppressed me. When I was able to see the truth, I got angry that I had wasted so many years with all these toxic emotions hidden deep in my heart. The truth is that the healing journey is messy; people experience a wide range of emotions. For me, decades of buried emotions erupted in full force like a volcano.

The only way to be free is to humble ourselves before the Lord, examine our hearts, and let the emotions surface. It's okay to grieve over the things that have been done and said against us. It's okay to grieve over the mistakes we have made. It is healthy to grieve for the things that we have done wrong against ourselves and against others; however, it is unhealthy to stay in that place of grief. Grieve. Confess. Receive God's forgiveness, and move on.

As I read Psalm 51 as a prayer, God took my grief from feeling sorry for myself to a healing grief where He had permission to heal my soul. The Bible says,

> But [God] continues to pour out more and more grace upon us. For it says, God resists you when you are proud but continually pours out grace when you are humble." ...Feel the pain of your sin, be sorrowful and weep! Let your joking around be

turned into mourning and your joy into deep humiliation. Be willing to be made low before the Lord and he will exalt you![87]

During my healing process, I attended an inner healing conference. This was a safe place for me. A lady who prayed for me did not know me or anything about my life, but it was as if she looked straight into my heart. She asked me to wrap my arms around her and when I did, I felt the Father's love completely overwhelmed me.

She told me there was a deep grief inside of me, and God was removing that grief. She whispered that God was doing a deep, deep healing in the core of my being. I was ugly crying as she held me. I physically felt a spirit of grief being pulled out of me. Experiences are hard to explain; however, since that moment I have never felt the heaviness of grief again. God is faithful. He promises to heal the wounds of every shattered heart,[88] and He supports and strengthens the humble.[89] This deliverance has enabled me to process my dad's death in a healthy way. I am confident that my dad is waiting for me in heaven along with my firstborn.

---

[87] James 4:6; 9-10 TPT
[88] Psalm 147:3
[89] Psalm 147:6

Let It Go

Have you ever done something to hurt someone, felt badly about it, and asked them to forgive you? Sometimes when people forgive us easily and freely, it is difficult to know what to do with such generosity. We are used to people holding a grudge and treating us horribly to "punish" us for our mistakes. Sometimes, we do the same thing. When someone does us wrong, we struggle to forgive. We want to tuck the grievance in our pocket and pull it out whenever necessary.

The truth is we cannot desire forgiveness for our wrongdoing, and yet withhold it from those who have done wrongs to us. If you want to receive forgiveness, you have to give forgiveness. Jesus said, "*And when you pray*, make sure you forgive the faults of others so that your Father in heaven will also forgive you."[90] The shame blame game keeps God out of our lives, and then we blame Him for our troubles. Have you ever heard someone say, "They are gonna be sorry they ever messed with me."? Do you see the toxicity of this thinking? Unforgiveness blocks our own forgiveness and halts God from moving in our lives.

---

[90] Matthew 6:14 TPT

Forgiveness is not easy, but it is necessary. When we offer others forgiveness, we are able to receive forgiveness. This then empowers us to live a confident life full of joy. Believe it or not, I had to forgive God. Why? I was mad at Him. I had blamed Him for every trauma that happened in my life. Thankfully, God can handle it when we come to Him raw and broken. I shouted. I screamed. I wept. I may have even thrown a fist or two in the air. With patient love, He waited for me to get it all out. Then, I felt His love cover me as I repented for believing the lie that He caused and allowed these sufferings in my life. I also asked God to forgive me for believing all the lies about His identity and character.

The second person I had to forgive was myself. Open doors of trauma and brokenness had led to promiscuity. I hated who I was; I hated what I had become. I took a lot of time forgiving myself for each and every thing that I hated about myself. I forgave myself for the lies I believed, helping me to release the toxic shame, the fear, and the self-hatred. I released the low self-esteem. I forgave myself fully and began the journey of loving who God created me to be.

Thirdly, I forgave each person who contributed to my grief. I forgave everything from the traumatic to the simplistic. Forgiveness doesn't give people an all-access card into our lives. In order to maintain healthy boundaries, some people are not safe for us. This is okay. Forgiveness is both a choice and a process. We often have to repeat the choice of forgiveness until the pain is gone, and the soul is healed.

As we grieve over the things that have been done to us and against us, we freely release the sins of the other person. This doesn't mean that they get away with what they have done. There are consequences to every action, but the consequences are not up to us. We must step aside and allow God to be God in this area. Our choice to forgive keeps bitterness from taking root and helps us to move forward in a healthy way.

Healing is a process. We have to let go of negative, resentful, and revengeful thoughts. Remember the dog that continued to lick his wounds? Here's what happens. We choose to forgive, and the wound begins to heal. Then something replays in our minds, and we begin to lick the wound. This slows down our healing process, and we become discouraged because we thought we had forgiven. For deep issues, the feeling of forgiveness comes in layers.

Ever notice that the negative things said to us are so much easier to remember? Sometimes the positive things have little to no impact because the lies play like a broken record in our heads. When our hearts are hurting, it's easier to believe the negative things about us. It takes more faith to believe the positive. It takes more faith to believe that God has a plan and a purpose for our lives when all we see are chaos and destruction. But God!

I had to choose to forgive those who spoke judgments over me. I also asked God to break every word curse spoken over me and release me from its power. I repented for holding bitterness and anger in my heart toward these people. Forgiveness begins with a choice. We choose to allow the blood of Jesus to wash away the offense. We give up our right for justice. Instead, we choose to trust God and allow Him to deal with the other person in His way and in His timing. Again, it's not always easy, but it's for our own good.

How do we let it go? We stop looking back. We stop licking our wounds. We allow ourselves the time to heal by going through the process of forgiveness. The pain that grips us begins to lose its hold. The longer we hold onto something, the stronger its power of destruction in our lives becomes. We have the choice to hold on or let go. We choose! Choose wisely.

UNQUALIFIED
CHAPTER 20

Unqualified
There was a time when I believed that my actions were too bad for the blood of Jesus to cover. The price He paid wasn't quite enough to handle my past. His blood couldn't possibly redeem and restore me. His blood was incapable of working all my bad into good for His glory. The voice in my head screamed, "You're unqualified. God can't use you! Who would listen to you? Don't follow your dream, Shannon. It's too late. You'll make a fool of yourself. No one will ever value what you have to say. You'll fall on your face in shame."

Lies. ALL LIES.

Sound familiar? This is how toxic Christians treat others. Satan uses the voices of others to point an accusing finger, and he torments us with thoughts of not being good enough. When we are treated like a misfit, an outcast, or unworthy of being part of a particular church, the door is wide open for Satan to step in and do what he does best – steal, kill, and destroy.

My problem was that I kept stuffing my emotions inside – like a hall closet whose door will barely stay shut. Something would happen, and I would take the emotion and throw it into the closet of my heart, shutting the door as quickly as possible. I'm guessing I'm not the only one to ever do this. Eventually, we have no choice but to clean that closet. When we first open the door, some stuff falls out on its own. When we look around, we've got one huge mess on our hands. That was so me! My emotions were one big fat mess.

Once everything is removed, we stare at the empty closet. For one moment, we ignore the mess around us and simply breathe. But then, the real work begins. We have to decide what we'll keep and what will be thrown away. We focus on one item at a time until the mess is gone. In the midst of the cleanup, it can be overwhelming. If you're anything like me, when you start a project it takes longer and requires more energy than expected. Nevertheless, if we choose to persevere, we will have an organized closet as well as evidence of stuff we no longer need. The same is true with our emotions. When we allow God to help us clean our hearts, He'll illuminate emotions we no longer need, people who really aren't our friends, and lies we have believed. He'll gladly take our emotional baggage and throw it in the fire.

Island of Misfit Toys

I have spoken to so many different people from different walks of life who have stated that they feel like something is wrong with them; they just don't fit in. It reminds me of the 1964 version of *Rudolph the Red Nosed Reindeer*[91]. In the holiday special, there was a place called the Island of Misfit Toys. All the broken, irregular, or imperfect toys were sent to this island. These toys were the discarded ones that no one else wanted. Have you ever heard the expression, "Welcome to the Island of Misfit Toys?" To me, it is a place metaphorically where we are sent or send ourselves when we feel like we are not good enough or have been discarded.

In the holiday special, the toys, along with Rudolph and his friends, sit around a small fire, looking up into the night sky with a skeptical hope that Santa will find a place for them to belong. They dream that their uniqueness will be of use. Of course, Santa does a Christmas miracle and finds a loving home for each of them! The toys can hardly believe that what they'd hoped and dreamed actually came to pass.

While I would never compare Santa Claus to God, the story provides a good illustration of redemption. God

---

[91] https://www.imdb.com/title/tt0058536/

created each of us uniquely beautiful, and He has the perfect place for us. There are people who will love us and allow us to function in our original design. Don't worry! Just like Santa helped the misfit toys, God will help us find the people who will be a blessing in our lives and will allow us to be a blessing in theirs!

Perfectly Imperfect

Why do I share so many painful and humiliating stories? If I have had these painful struggles, how many others have struggled with the same emotions and feelings? I want you to see how I journeyed through my brokenness to find wholeness. There is life, hope, and joy for the broken, wounded, and rejected.

I thought I had to be perfect before God could use me. Originally, I believed the lie that my sin was too big and that God could never use me again. I carried that around with me for many years. I didn't truly believe Jesus could forgive that "one" sin. Do you have thoughts like that? You think, "Yes, I know Jesus forgives, but this one thing I did was too bad. If anyone ever found out about it, I couldn't endure it." Why do we think and believe this? Toxic Christianity has taught us this.

Here's the truth: God has used me time and again – even as He was healing my own heart. I heard Him tell me to reach out to others in the very areas in which I needed Him to move in my life. I knew what I needed. I needed help with my daughter and needed God to move in her life. Out of the blue, I received a phone call from a young woman close in age to my daughter. I mentored her for about a year and walked with her through a difficult time. God is faithful, and she is doing great!

As I continued to give God my "yes," He sent people to me. It didn't matter that I didn't feel qualified or ready; God said I was ready. I never announced I wanted to help people who were wounded and shamed, but they started to come. I never said my heart was toward those who felt like misfits and outcasts; they found me.

God is funny. He will often enable us to help others and use the very words that come out of our mouths to bring hope and healing into our own hearts. I grew and benefited from the relationships with these precious ones. Even though I was judged as unworthy and unqualified by some, the Lord found me trustworthy. As my daughter saw the many changes in my life, we began to rebuild our relationship.

Jesus' Specialty is the Unqualified

Because of our wounds and our past, we tend to think we are automatically disqualified. People treat us as though we are contagious and confirm the lie that we are unfit misfits for their circles. The truth is that when we have been forgiven much, we in turn love much. We are perfect candidates for God to get all the glory for things that happen in us and through us. The world tends to look for those who have natural talents and abilities, but God has a different perspective. God used His Word to expose the lie I believed about being unqualified.

God's Calling

Brothers and sisters, consider who you were when God called you *to salvation*. Not many of you were wise scholars by human standards, nor were many of you in positions of power. Not many of you were considered the elite *when you answered God's call*. But God chose those whom the world considers foolish to shame those who think they are wise, and God chose the puny and powerless to shame the high and mighty. He chose the lowly, the laughable in the world's eyes—nobodies—so that he would shame the somebodies. For he chose what is regarded as insignificant in order to supersede what is regarded as prominent, so that there would be no place for prideful boasting in God's presence. *For it is not from man that we draw our life* but from God as we are being joined to Jesus, the Anointed One. And now he is our God-given wisdom, our virtue, our holiness, and our redemption. And this fulfills what is written: If anyone boasts, let him only boast in all that the Lord has done![92]

The simple beauty is that in spite of all our shortcomings and failures, God gathers up all the bruised and broken pieces of our lives and creates something glorious. He is the master Craftsman and Creator. He makes all things beautiful. The hardest thing for those who are wounded, hidden, and filled with shame is coming out of the cave, choosing to be humble, and letting God's light shine on those painful areas.

Be forewarned: there may be some criticism and ugly remarks. Some people will resist our wholeness and despise our success. That's okay. Our identity is in Christ, not the onlookers or naysayers. We can trust Jesus with our heart. We can trust Him with our wounds. We can trust Him with our pain. We will not be put to shame or

---

[92] 1 Corinthians 1:26-31 TPT

disappointed.[93] In fact, God is looking for those who know they need Him – those who don't want to do anything without Him.

Why is that? Why does God love to work with the humble? First, let's look at pride. Satan was cast out of heaven because of pride. People who are arrogant and filled with pride knowingly or unknowingly align with Satan as their father; however, the humble look to God as their Father.

You, Beloved, are not inferior to others. You are not a loser. You are not a second-rate Christian to those who think they are the "elite." Everyone sins. Everyone falls short. That's why we need a savior. People see sin in varying degrees from small to huge. But to God, sin is sin.

Jesus Called You Qualified
The things we have done do not surprise or catch Jesus off guard. He lives outside of time and sees the beginning from the end. He knows that we will fall yet still chooses us. You are chosen! You are loved. You are accepted. God has a plan and a purpose for YOU. During my senior year of high school, God gave me a dream. It impacted me so

---

[93] Romans 10:11

much that when I awoke, I immediately repented and told God that I was His. I gave Him permission to use me however He wanted. Here's the thing: Jesus knew I was pregnant at the time; I did not. The manifestation of that dream stopped when others found out I was pregnant. Jesus said one thing; toxic Christianity said another. Unfortunately, I listened to toxic Christians believing that the dream God gave me was nothing more than a fairy tale. Therefore, I delved back into darkness.

When God gives you a dream, He knows the good, the bad, and the ugly before He gave you the assignment. God's call on each of our lives is irrevocable, and He never rescinds it.[94]

> Since we are now joined to Christ, we have been given the treasures of redemption by his blood—the total cancellation of our sins—all because of the cascading riches of his grace. This superabundant grace is already powerfully working in us, releasing within us all forms of wisdom and practical understanding. And through the revelation of the Anointed One, he unveiled his secret desires to us—the hidden mystery of his long-range plan, which he was delighted to implement from

---

[94] Romans 11:29

the very beginning of time. And because of God's unfailing purpose, this detailed plan will reign supreme through every period of time until the fulfillment of all the ages finally reaches its climax—when God makes all things new in all of heaven and earth through Jesus Christ.

Through our union with Christ we too have been claimed by God as his own inheritance. Before we were even born, he gave us our destiny; that we would fulfill the plan of God who always accomplishes every purpose and plan in his heart.[95]

And by the blood of his cross, everything in heaven and earth is brought back to himself—*back to its original intent, restored to innocence again!*[96]
(Emphasis added)

It's the power of His love that brings our life back to His original intent. God is bringing the misfits, the outcasts, and those rejected by the church back to His original plan for them. As this happens, it becomes a catalyst for change in the entire Body of Christ. A lot of adjustments need to be made in Christian culture; nevertheless, I'm

---

[95] Ephesians 1:7-11 TPT
[96] Colossians 1:20 TPT

confident as we all get a revelation of God's love, it will bring transformation.

I'm willing to do my part. I yielded to the healing process of the Lord and allowed Him free reign in my life. Are you ready to surrender and allow the Lord to bind up your broken heart? Consider this: we use our GPS to get us to our destination. When we take a wrong turn, it reroutes us to get us back on track. The same is true with our lives. We may have tried to take short-cuts that resulted in detours, road blocks, or construction zones. We may have made wrong choices that took us way off course, but if we allow God to reroute us, we will STILL reach our destination and fulfill our purpose.

It is time to rekindle those passions and dreams in your heart! They have been dormant for far too long. Dormant doesn't mean dead! There's still hope for those dreams and visions to become reality! It doesn't matter what someone else has said to you about your sin. When you repent, Jesus throws your sin into the sea of forgetfulness. This world needs the answers and love that you have to offer. There are people waiting for you on the other side. You just need to choose to take the first step. You are worth the journey. Your purpose in Christ is worth the process. Your life makes a difference.

REFORMERS AND REPAIRERS
CHAPTER 21

Reformers and Reformation
Throughout church history, there have always been religious leaders, average church attendees, and reformers. The reformers are those who follow the way of Jesus with passion. They are fearless believers that are catalysts for change. Their aim is to challenge the status quo through love and truth. Do not be deceived: one person can make a difference and heed a call for change.

Many people are feeling the need for change within the church; unfortunately, most people think the task is impossible. Denominations are divided by different doctrinal beliefs, yet Christians are supposed to be known by our unity and our love. Love is not a weak, flimsy emotion. Love brings strength and unity. There is power in love. God is coming for a powerful, pure, united body of believers, His bride. One body! Change is inevitable. The way we currently "DO" church does not equate with our calling to "BE" the church.

Throughout history, God sent prophets to remind His people of who we are meant to be. Every time the church becomes too institutionalized, God sends reformers to speak truth and reroute us back to the heart of God. Presently, the Church needs a course correction.

"In 1517 [Martin] Luther penned a document attacking the Catholic Church's corrupt practice of selling "indulgences" to absolve sin. His '95 Theses,' which propounded two central beliefs—that the Bible is the central religious authority and that humans may reach salvation only by their faith and not by their deeds—was to spark the Protestant Reformation."[97]

Reformation is from a heart of love, not rebellion. The Protestant Reformation began with a hunger for God, truth, and societal transformation. Isn't that what we want? Isn't that what our hearts cry out for? We desperately want someone to show us the way. Our hearts yearn for truth that bring transformation, and we desire to live life authentically and abundantly.

When it is time for change there will be a cry of resistance. Those comfortable in their positions do not want to give up the authority that they have. My thoughts

---

[97] https://www.history.com/topics/reformation/martin-luther-and-the-95-theses (1/29/2019)

go to the American Revolutionary War when the 13 colonies wanted to be free from their "mother" England.

In a very short review, the colonists rebelled against the British government. Britain was demanding that the colonies pay higher taxes. Feeling oppressed, the colonists protested this taxation without representation. Relations between the local British army and the colonists continued to escalate. Great Britain did not want to give up authority in the new world. The colonies united to make a single government and signed the Declaration of Independence in 1776; however, in order to obtain freedom, they had to engage in war.[98]

The thought of 13 colonies against the British Empire seemed impossible. Britain never expected a bunch of farming colonists with no military training to overtake the British army. Fifty states later, we know that the settlers did gain their freedom from Britain.

It doesn't matter what the enemy looks like or how strong he is, God's plan and purpose will prevail! God will not allow His sheep to continue to be mistreated, mishandled, and abused. Reformation isn't easy. We'll have to fight the enemy of our souls to obtain it. We may

---

[98] https://en.wikipedia.org/wiki/American_Revolutionary_War (1/29/2019)

not like it at first, and it may make us uncomfortable. So, let us embrace what God is doing in us as well as what He wants to do through us!

> 'This is what I will do in the last days —I will pour out my Spirit on everybody and cause your sons and daughters to prophesy, and your young men will see visions, and your old men will experience dreams *from God*. The Holy Spirit will come upon all my servants, men and women alike, and they will prophesy. I will reveal startling signs and wonders in the sky above and mighty miracles on the earth below. Blood and fire and pillars of clouds will appear. For the sun will be turned dark and the moon blood-red before that great and awesome appearance of the day of the Lord. But everyone who calls on the name of the Lord will be saved.'"[99]

God wants to move on all flesh – not only those comfortable and safe inside the four walls of a church building. God is pouring out His Spirit on men and women, regardless of age, sexual orientation, and religious beliefs. Everybody means every human, not

---

[99] *Acts 2:17-21 TPT*

only the elite or platform ministers within Christianity. God sent Jesus to heal the brokenhearted and to bind up their wounds. Our humanity qualifies us to become healed and serve with purity and power through the cross of Jesus.

Repairer of the Breach

As I awoke on the morning of August 13, 2015, the phrase "Repairer of the Breach" went through my mind. It was so loud and clear that I thought it was audible even though I knew I was alone. My curiosity was peaked, so I went to the Bible. In Isaiah 58, the Lord says, "And your ancient ruins shall be rebuilt; you shall raise up the foundation of [buildings that have laid waste for] many generations; and you shall be called repairer of the breach, restorer of Streets to Dwell in."[100]

The context of Isaiah 58 is about fasting. The first half is about "religious people who are full of sin. They have an external religion, which allows them to live in rebellion against God. And such people are not easily convicted of sin."[101] These religious people do rituals caring only about the external. The second half of the chapter is about people who are fasting with the right heart motive.

---

[100] Isaiah 58:12 AMPC
[101] https://www.studylight.org/commentaries/spe/isaiah-58.html

These are the ones who care about matters of the heart and listen to the cries of those around them. As I read the chapter, I felt the Lord was talking to me about the emotional needs of the wounded and rejected.

God's desire is to connect the generations. At present, it seems that there is a lack of unity and understanding between the old and the young. The older generation has trouble relating to the younger generation and vice versa. In the shift that is coming, I believe that those who yield to God will see a bridge that will close the gap between the age groups and empower us to move forward in unity. The older generation can offer life experience and wisdom while the younger generation can provide fresh, new ideas with unlimited energy. Both are needed and necessary for what God has planned.

Second, God revealed that He is repairing the relationship between the church and the bruised sheep. Even though the task looks difficult, God's heart is to heal the Body of Christ from the religious leaders to the outcasts.

God is preparing people who will be willing to step in as peacemakers between the rejected and the leaders as well as help with the doctrinal disconnect between denominations. These people are pioneers and will be called repairers of the breach. It's time to redeem and reconcile what the enemy has stolen from the Church.

Have you seen the movie, *The Intern*, with Robert De Niro, and Anne Hathaway? You may be rolling your eyes at another movie example, but they make such good illustrations! "Seventy-year-old widower Ben Whittaker [Robert De Niro] has discovered that retirement isn't all it's cracked up to be. Seizing an opportunity to get back in the game, he becomes a senior intern at an online fashion site, founded and run by Jules Ostin [Anne Hathaway]."[102]

"Jules [is] a tireless, driven, demanding, dynamic workaholic. Ben is made her intern, but this is a nominal role - she doesn't intend to give him work, and it is just window dressing. However, Ben proves to be quite useful and, more than that, a source of support and wisdom."[103] It's fun to watch how the two generations have such different views, yet as they get to know each other a mutual respect grows. They each take the time to listen to the other. The movie illustrates the healing of the generational gap as problems are tackled together resulting in success.

---

[102] https://www.imdb.com/title/tt2361509/ (1/30/2019)
[103] https://www.imdb.com/title/tt2361509/

Outcasts with A Heart for God

Rahab is a wonder woman in the Bible to me. Her full story is told in Joshua 2:1-24 and in Joshua 6:1-25. She was a prostitute who had outrageous faith and believed in the God of Israel. Her life took a dramatic turn full of intrigue and bravery when she hid two of Israel's spies in her home. When her city's soldiers questioned her about the spies, she lied and said the Israelites had left. Rahab then told the spies how her people had heard the stories of the great exploits of the God of Israel. Her people were afraid of the Israelite's God. Then, Rahab pleaded for her life and for her family.

> This woman is listed in the Hebrews 11 Hall of Faith. "Faith provided a way of escape for Rahab the prostitute, avoiding the destruction of the unbelievers, because she received the Hebrew spies in peace."[104] This prostitute was named as an ancestor in Jesus' genealogy.[105]

Rahab placed a scarlet cord in her window to help the Israelites know which family to save. The scarlet cord represents a type and shadow of the redeeming blood of Jesus – the blood saves, the blood protects, and the blood redeems. No one would have ever thought that Rahab

---

[104] Hebrews 11:31 TPT
[105] Matthew 1:5

would be honored and qualified to be in the lineage of Jesus. But with God in the picture, anything is possible.

Another Biblical hero that was once an outcast is David. The Lord sent the prophet, Samuel, to Jesse's house to anoint one of his sons as king. Jesse brought seven of his sons to Samuel, but the Lord had not chosen any of them. Samuel asked Jesse if he had any other sons. Jesse then remembers his son, David, who was tending the sheep. Even though David had killed a lion and a bear while protecting the sheep, Jesse didn't find him worthy or qualified to be considered as the future king of Israel to replace Saul. So, Samuel made Jesse and his sons wait until David arrived. At first sight, Samuel knew God had chosen David to be king. He took a horn of oil and anointed David in the presence of his brothers; the Spirit of the Lord came upon David from that day forward.[106]

To make a long story short, David was an excellent musician. King Saul would ask for David to come play for him. Even though David has been anointed by the Lord to be the king of Israel, he faithfully served King Saul. But the king became jealous of David, and David fled to the cave of Adullam. David was now an outlaw; nevertheless, he was still a leader. All the men who were in distress,

---

[106] 1 Samuel 16

debt or discontented (bitter) gathered around David. David became the leader of about four hundred men who were considered outcasts.[107]

In 1 Samuel 30, David and his mighty men returned from war to find their camp had been raided. No one was killed, but all the wives and children had been taken captive. All the men wept and grew angry toward David. "David was greatly distressed because the men were talking of stoning him; each one was bitter in spirit because of his sons and daughters. But David found strength in the LORD his God."[108] There was no one to encourage him. There was no shoulder for David to cry on. There was no one to listen to his heartbreaking story; he was alone. In his darkest moment, David chose to encourage himself in the Lord. How did he do that?

David knew God intimately. He didn't blame God for all the things that went wrong in his life. David wrote many of psalms in the Bible. I believe that David reminded himself that God was with him when he killed the lion, the bear, and even Goliath. *Maybe* David said something like this:

---

[107] 1 Samuel 22
[108] 1 Samuel 30:6 NIV

"The Lord is my justice, my shield, and my peace. The Lord is healing and merciful. The Lord always provides for me. He is my victorious hand; He is my Shepherd. The Lord is love, patient, and kind. He cares about me, and He has never forsaken me. The Lord is my deliverer and He is jealous over me. He is the light of my life and will never fail me. The Lord knows my heart and because God does not fail, I will not fail."

After David had encouraged himself in the Lord, something interesting happened. The men united with him once again. David asked the Lord if he should pursue the people who raided his camp. God said yes. Not only did David and his men recover everything that had been taken, but also they captured livestock and other things from the Amalekites. David took his rightful place as king shortly after this event.

Later, David committed adultery and had the woman's husband killed. His son, Absalom, wanted to kill him and take the throne for himself. Regardless of David's sin or traumatic events, David kept a humble heart and repented before the Lord. He always ran to God, not from God. "God said of him, 'I have found in David, son of Jesse, a man who always pursues my heart and will accomplish all that I have destined him to do.'"[109]

You may feel like a misfit. You may feel unqualified. But today is a new day. Let hope begin to stir again in your heart. See the light shining at the end of the dark tunnel. There are more FOR you than those that are against you. All of heaven is cheering you on! You have what it takes to press through your pain and be restored to your rightful place.

---

[109] Acts 13:22b TPT

CONFIDENT IN YOUR SKIN
CHAPTER 22

Come Out of the Cave
It's time for a perspective shift. It's time to stop believing the lies that we are worthless garbage. God doesn't create garbage. He has a plan for each of us. In the areas where we feel broken, God desires to put the pieces back together. Don't get it twisted; God uses the very ones that the church has discarded. We are in the perfect position for our destiny to unfold. I want to share with you a very private and personal prophetic word that was spoken over me. Even though most of the traumas I experienced were more than 20-25 years ago, I've still kept myself hidden.

I was taking a class through Donna Partow's Women's Empowerment University. One of the assignments was to create a vision board. Donna was going to prophetically pray over the submitted boards. When Donna prayed for me, I was driving down I-95 heading to a makeup class for the weekend. As Donna prayed, her words impacted me so deeply that I had to pull off of the road. Tears were streaming, mascara was running, and my eyes were burning. I could hardly breathe. She barely even touched what was on my vision board; nevertheless, she said exactly what I needed to hear. Her words were potent and powerfully accurate as they pierced straight through to the depths of my soul.

Donna having no prior knowledge of my background said,

> "Shannon, I'm so proud of you! Rediscovering your beauty! You're rediscovering your beauty which is potent and powerful. Maybe that scared you. Maybe being beautiful wasn't always safe. I don't know what happened, but you are very beautiful. Something happened that made the power and the potency of your beauty maybe not the safest thing. You, like many people who come [to Women's Empowerment University], made a decision that your beauty was too potent, too powerful. In a sense, you have marred your own beauty. Women do this; we mar our own beauty, but that's over.

> "That is over! It's a season for joy and laughter and love...romance and delight. It's time to embrace the power and the potency of your beauty and to be safe with it. But I just want to say, come out, come out. Come out, wherever you are. It's safe

to be beautiful now. Come out, come out wherever you are. Healed and restored. A family healthy, healed, and restored starts with YOU healthy, healed, and restored. That's where it starts, with YOU setting the example. There you go, confirmation, not safe. Well... you know what? It's safe. So come out!"

You may be wondering what Donna meant by marring your beauty. I added a bunch of weight, believing that it would keep me safe from myself and from others. The truth is it worked for a while, but then the added weight didn't make a huge difference. Through this prophetic word, God was telling me that I was healthy and whole. It was safe to come out of my cave, to be the woman He created me to be. The work in the wilderness was complete. I was healthy and whole. Anytime a prophetic word is given publicly, we have the ability to receive it for ourselves even if we are not the initially intended recipient. I want you to read what God led Donna to share with me as if God is speaking to you. It's safe. It's safe to come out. It's safe to be you. It's safe to beYOUtiful.

I am still a work in progress, and so is my weight. I know that God is asking me to finally obey Him in this area. I'm sure that I will be rebelliously obedient until I have conquered it once and for all. I have been on a roller

coaster ride in this area since my daughter was born. I'd lose some weight, feel panic, sabotage myself, and gain it back. Even though I hate the added weight and the way it makes me feel, it is a comfortable cloak of false safety. #truestory #transparency
#whatisyourcloak

We've already established that I am a movie buff; however, I am especially fond of superhero movies. As I watch the superhero movies, I imagine that these superheroes are what the church is supposed to look like. Superheroes fight against evil and help those in need. If superheroes don't rise to the occasion, villains take over and chaos reigns. This is true in the spiritual kingdom war as well. Good versus evil. Heaven versus Hell. If we are not healthy and whole, we can't fight alongside those who need us to help them be victorious.

My favorite superhero is Wonder Woman. To me, she represents strong women of faith. "Power. Grace. Wisdom. Wonder." These words were used on the 2017 advertising posters for the Wonder Woman movie. I loved that! In the movie, "Diana, princess of the Amazons, trained to be an unconquerable warrior. Raised on a sheltered island paradise, when a pilot crashes on their shores and tells of a massive conflict raging in the outside world, Diana leaves her home, convinced she can stop the threat. Fighting alongside man in a war to end all wars, Diana will discover her full powers and her true destiny."[110]

The enemy knew Diana's full potential even before she realized it herself. This is true in our lives as well! The enemy of our souls knows our true purpose and potential, which is why he fights to keep each of us broken and defeated. He fears the damage we would cause to the kingdom of darkness. Since the fall of Adam and Eve, women have not been allowed their rightful place in the world or in Body of Christ, but God is shifting that. Throughout scripture, Jesus was a champion of women, and their strengths are especially needed in this hour.

Personally, I believe Wonder Woman is a prophetic symbol for women to realize our strength and beauty. I'm not only referring to physical beauty but also the beauty of walking in the grace and power of who God called us to be. God is speaking; He wants us to dream, imagine, and do what we were created to do. You are created for greatness. Don't allow the lies of religion and toxic Christians to tell you what you can't do; listen to Jesus as He tells you what you can do.

---

[110] https://www.imdb.com/title/tt0451279/

Birthed on Purpose

Maybe you weren't planned. Maybe people said you were a mistake. Maybe you were conceived at a bad time for your parents. Maybe you were the result of a one night stand or rape. Regardless of the circumstances surrounding your conception, God designed you in your mother's womb. He desired you, and He has purpose for you. King David, the man after God's own heart, said this about his own birth:

> Lord, I have been a sinner from birth, from the moment my mother conceived me. I know that you delight to set your truth deep in my spirit. So come into the hidden places of my heart and teach me wisdom.[111]

You Know All About Me

> Lord, you know everything there is to know about me. You perceive every movement of my heart and soul, and you understand my every thought before it even enters my mind. You are so intimately aware of me, Lord. You read my heart like an open book and you know all the words I'm about to speak before I even start a sentence! You know every step I will take before my journey even begins.

---

[111] Psalm 51:5-6 TPT

You've gone into my future to prepare the way, and in kindness you follow behind me to spare me from the harm of my past. With your hand of love upon my life, you impart a blessing to me.

This is just too wonderful, deep, and incomprehensible! Your understanding of me brings me wonder and strength. Where could I go from your Spirit? Where could I run and hide from your face? If I go up to heaven, you're there! If I go down to the realm of the dead, you're there too! If I fly into the radiant sunset, you're there waiting! Wherever I go, your hand will guide me; your strength will empower me. It's impossible to disappear from you or to ask the darkness to hide me, for your presence is everywhere, bringing light into my night. There is no such thing as darkness with you. The night, to you, is as bright as the day; there's no difference between the two.

You formed my innermost being, shaping my delicate inside and my intricate outside, and wove them all together in my mother's womb. I thank you, God, for making me so mysteriously complex! Everything you do is marvelously breathtaking. It

simply amazes me to think about it! How thoroughly you know me, Lord! You even formed every bone in my body when you created me in the secret place, carefully, skillfully shaping me from nothing to something. You saw who you created me to be before I became me! Before I'd ever seen the light of day, the number of days you planned for me were already recorded in your book.

Every single moment you are thinking of me! How precious and wonderful to consider that you cherish me constantly in your every thought! O God, your desires toward me are more than the grains of sand on every shore! When I awake each morning, you're still with me.[112] (Emphasis added)

Not only did God lovingly form us and breathe life into our mother's womb when we were conceived, but also He picked the exact time in history for us to walk the earth. He chose the geographical location of where we would be born. He picked the color of our skin. He chose our nationality. He handpicked our personality. He even chose the family into which we would be born. The

---

[112] Psalm 139:1-18 TPT

Apostle Paul said,

> The true God is the Creator of all things. He
> is the owner and Lord of the heavenly
> realm and the earthly realm, and he
> doesn't live in man-made temples. He
> supplies life and breath and all things to
> every living being. He doesn't lack a thing
> that we mortals could supply for him, for
> he has all things and everything he needs.
> From one man, Adam, he made every man
> and woman and every race of humanity,
> and he spread us over all the earth. He sets
> the boundaries of people and nations,
> determining their appointed times in
> history. He has done this so that every
> person would long for God, feel their way
> to him, and find him—for he is the God
> who is easy to discover! **It is through him
> that we live and function and have our
> identity**; just as your own poets have said,
> 'Our lineage comes from him.[113]
> (Emphasis added)

This is how involved God is in our lives. God put us into
our families exactly when He wanted. Were you born into
a family filled with blessings? Celebrate what He has
done. Maybe you were born into a difficult family full of

---

[113]Acts 17:24-28 TPT

brokenness, chaos, and bad habits from previous generations, then be the one to turn your family's curses into blessings. God put everything we need on the inside of us to change the circumstances surrounding us. All He asks is that we partner with Him. We are co-laborers with Christ. He longs to turn curses into blessings, break downs into breakthroughs, and the enemy's tests into His glory.

Know Your Identity, It Brings Confidence

The most effective way to move forward and be confident is to know your identity. I'm not talking about arrogance, but rather a true confidence in knowing **who you are** and **Whose you are**. God does not create junk. Everything He creates is beautiful. EVERYTHING! Let the Lord redefine you. Let His opinion of you become the one that matters. It may take a while to grasp and accept what He says about you. That's okay! But know this: God is love! What He says about you will look like love, sound like love, and feel like love. If the words you hear do not produce faith, hope, or love, those aren't words from our Heavenly Father.

There is power in a name. The most powerful name in the world is Jesus. However, Jesus wants us to understand the power in our own names. When I didn't know my identity, I defined myself by what other people said about me both positively and negatively. I also knew what I thought about myself, but I needed to wipe the slate clean. What does God say about me?

God planned each of our names. As I stated before, Shannon means possessor of wisdom. When I looked up my complete name Shannon Denise Hair, adding my middle name and my married last name, the Lord highlighted a few things to me.

Shannon Denise Hair, my full name, the Lord highlighted a few things to me. When someone speaks the name Shannon Denise Hair, the following decree is being proclaimed: a possessor of wisdom; inspired of God, the coolest person in the world; long-lasting.

Take some time and search out the meaning of your name. Our names bring revelation to our character. If your name doesn't seem very positive, ask the Lord for a new name. He changed many names in the Bible. Jacob was known as a deceiver, but God changed Jacob's name to Israel, one who wrestles with God, the Lord will prevail.

We have a natural identity, but we also have an identity hidden in Christ because we are one with Him. We are the Bride of Christ. We are priests and royalty. We take on all of Jesus' attributes. We are of Christ-like nobility and virtue. We are filled with grace, salvation, deliverance, and healing (sozo). We are filled with the same power that raised Christ from the dead; we are filled with the presence of God Himself. God has empowered us with His anointing. We are co-rulers with Christ.

No other human in history is created like you. Each of us is made in the image of God.[114] Since we are created in God's image, our uniqueness is a special part of God Himself. Think about it. We each have a unique DNA and fingerprint. If necessary, our fingerprints are what can be used to identify us. No two persons are alike. Nevertheless, complete emotional healing is crucial for walking in our identity and pressing toward what God created us to do.

---

[114] Genesis 1:27

SALT & LIGHT
CHAPTER 23

I n my search for the modern day church of Acts, I began to travel and go places as the Lord led me. It felt like I was on a personal, spiritual treasure hunt; everywhere God sent me I found a spiritual nugget of buried treasure. He was giving me answers and providing me with a visual example at each place. I was surrounded by people who were walking in the manifest presence of God. I was fascinated by the love that I saw. These people genuinely loved each other and had servant hearts.

During Patricia King's Bootcamp in 2016, they shared this story. A group of Christians went to a porn convention and set up a booth. The Christians gave away different colored bracelets; they spoke something beautiful and positive to every person who came to the booth. This became the most popular booth at the convention. Here is what I learned: They never once attacked people with Bible scriptures or even used the name of Jesus. They never told them they were sinning or that they were going to hell. The Christians went to take light and love in a dark place. There was no judgment. When they showed up, so did Love; God is love. They simply loved people. When Love shows up, lives are changed.

Christians stepping out of their comfort zone to go to a porn convention for the distinct purpose of showing love is not something the majority of Christians in churches would be willing to do. These people didn't pretend to love or have an agenda. Their desire was to demonstrate the love of God. We cannot give other people love when we haven't received love. We cannot give love if we don't love ourselves. We cannot give what we do not possess.

Why am I stressing this? Because I know what it feels like to be an outcast. I know what it feels like to be rejected and not wanted as part of a church group. I know what it feels like to be shamed because of sin. I know what it feels like to be lost and alone, thinking all hope is gone. But Jesus left the 99 to find the one. Maybe reading this book is His way of reaching out and finding you. He's calling out to you desiring for you to come and follow Him.

As we are healed from our wounds, we begin to see and experience the Biblical Jesus; then, we are able to walk in love for others. We can go forward in God-confidence to be the salt and light in the earth.

Your lives are like salt among the people. But if you, like salt, become bland, how can your 'saltiness' be restored? Flavorless salt is good for nothing and will be thrown out and trampled on by others.

"Your lives light up the world. Let others see your light from a distance, for how can you hide a city that stands on a hilltop? And who would light a lamp and then hide it in an obscure place? Instead, it's placed where everyone in the house can benefit from its light. So don't hide your light! Let it shine brightly before others, so that the commendable things you do will shine as light upon them, and then they will give their praise to your Father in heaven.[115]

I am a saltaholic. I have always loved an excess of salt on my food. Sweet and salty is even better! Salt makes me very thirsty. What is the purpose of salt? Salt is used as a seasoning and a preservative. It can also be used as a disinfectant. Salt means wisdom. Flavorless salt means foolish. When we eat something salty it makes us thirsty. Like I said, the amount of salt I use does make me very thirsty. Stay with me here. Jesus said...

---

[115] Matthew 5:13-16 TPT

"All you thirsty ones, come to me! Come to me and drink! Believe in me so that rivers of living water will burst out from within you, flowing from your innermost being, just like the Scripture says!"[116]

Remember when we read the scriptures about the woman at the well? These are the words that Jesus spoke to her...

"If you drink from Jacob's well you'll be thirsty again and again, but if anyone drinks the living water I give them, they will never thirst again and will be forever satisfied! For when you drink the water I give you it becomes a gushing fountain of the Holy Spirit, springing up and flooding you with endless life!"[117]

As we are healed from our wounds, we are able to experience a personal relationship with Jesus. Our lives are transformed, and we begin to look like Jesus on the inside out. People become thirsty for what we have. Why would Jesus use salt and light together? I read in the footnotes of The Passion Translation Bible that it was a common practice in the time of Jesus to put salt on the

---

[116] John 7:37-38 TPT
[117] John 14:13-14 TPT

wick of a lamp to increase its brightness. It says, the "salt of wisdom will make our lights shine even brighter."[118]

Do our lives cause others to thirst for Living Water? When was the last time you watched someone's life and became thirsty for what they had? Not in a material sense, but you were drawn to their love, their uniqueness? Seriously, take the time to think about it. This is missing from most of our church culture.

My husband has a friend that he goes camping with, and this guy comes close to what I am talking about. People are naturally drawn to him; everyone feels accepted and comfortable around him. He judges no one. People can't quite put their finger on his uniqueness. I told him that he is a leader, and God has something special for him to do with his life. He is already quite accomplished by the world's standards, yet humble. He and his wife show genuine kindness and respect to everyone.

Remember, God gives each of us a choice. He never pushes anyone. He opens the door and invites us on a

---

[118] Eduard Schweizer, The Good News According to Matthew, Atlanta: John Knox Press, 1975. W.A. Elwell and P.W. Comfort, Tyndale Bible Dictionary, Wheaton, Ill.: Tyndale House, Tyndale reference library, 2001, Lamp, Lampstand. 797-8.

healing journey. The healing portion of the journey is only the first part. Now that my wilderness season is over, I am no longer willing to hang around where I feel tolerated but want to be connected with others where I am celebrated. We all have a tribe of people that we are to be part of, the right fit. In this tribe, there is genuine love for one another.

Real life is not meant to be serious all the time. Ecclesiastes Chapter 3 tells us that there is a time for everything: "A time to weep and a time to laugh, a time to mourn and a time to dance."[119] There's a time to focus on the wounds to gain healing, and there's a time to step away and have some fun. It reminds me of the original Karate Kid movie. Mr. Miyagi told Daniel, "Better learn balance. Balance is key. Balance good, karate good. Everything good. Balance bad, better pack up, go home. Understand?"[120] What Mr. Miyagi was saying is, "Balance is a double meaning word, you need balance to stand up and not fall, but you need balance in your life areas, or else your life will become unstable."[121]

The early church was a tribe. They prayed together; they

---

[119] ECCLESIASTES 3:4 NIV
[120] http://www.motivateamazebegreat.com/2015/12/20-mr-miyagi-inspirational-quotes-wisdom.html (2/5/19)
[121] http://www.motivateamazebegreat.com/2015/12/20-mr-miyagi-inspirational-quotes-wisdom.html (2/5/19)

read the Word together. They broke bread together; they fellowshipped together. They lived life together. They didn't sit for an hour once a week and barely talk to each other. Where they went people were healed, devils were cast out, dead were raised. They challenged each other, spoke truth to each other, and encouraged each other. I don't know about you, but these are my goals. This is not dull living! Imagine the thrill if we laid hands on a friend that was dying of cancer, and God instantly healed them! That's real! That's fun!

There are times in life when we feel like a fish out of water. Sometimes this feeling is an indication that it is time for us to move on. For instance, I worked for a church that ended up merging with another church for two years. I felt like the Lord advised me to step away when the church closed before it merged with the other congregation. Unfortunately, I was disobedient. When God tells us to move forward and we choose to stay, it usually brings unnecessary problems and heartaches. It is important for us to find mutually beneficial relationships and alliances. Everyone deserves to be celebrated, not merely tolerated. There are people who will love you and accept you for who you are; the key is to allow God to direct you to them.

MIRROR, MIRROR
CHAPTER 24

Warning! I'm getting really real here. You have read about things that I have overcome as well as my journey with the Lord. Honestly, I have pretty much been "rebelliously obedient" through most of it. Yes, you read that right, rebelliously obedient. It's my own term that I use to describe myself.

I was rebelliously obedient every time God asked me to go work somewhere I didn't want to go. I was rebelliously obedient every time He asked me to humble myself, and do something I didn't want to do. The journey becomes even more difficult when we resist God every step of the way. The problem was that I was willing, but I didn't want to. Contradictory? Possibly, but it's the truth.

This reminds me of the father of the demoniac in Mark 9:24, "Immediately the boy's father exclaimed, 'I do believe; help me overcome my unbelief!'". This person believed a little bit and needed help to fully believe. The father wanted to fully believe but couldn't get there on his own.

I was a little willing to be obedient because I wanted the victory at the end of the journey. My eyes were set on the dream, on the freedom that came from the healing process. Only, I didn't want to do what it took to get there. Every time I needed to take a step that was uncomfortable or stretched me, I went forward like a child in a tantrum, kicking and screaming.

Let me give you an example of a child being rebelliously obedient. One day a little boy came in from playing outside, and he was extremely energetic. His mom told him it was time for dinner and to wash his hands. The boy didn't want to go wash his hands because they were having broccoli for dinner. He hated broccoli. However, he finally washed his hands and went into the kitchen. The little boy told his mom he wasn't hungry and didn't want to sit at the table. The mom told her son to sit down. The boy was sassy and resistant until his mother in full out Mom-Tone said, "Sit down, now!" The boy dramatically slams himself into the chair and said, "I may be sitting down on the outside, but I am standing up on the inside." He did what he was told but not willingly – rebelliously obedient.

God and I have played tug-of-war quite a bit. I think that is what made my journey longer. I am so glad God is patient and has a sense of humor. He has to have one since I'm His child! I've often laughed and reminded Him that He created me! No, I'm not being disrespectful to a holy God. He enjoys having fun with us.

One day the Lord said to me very clearly, "Shannon, you have lost your childlike faith." It was one of those statements that pierced me straight through the heart because of the truth of these words. Man, oh man, the person (me) that loves to laugh and have fun had become too serious. Like I said, the journey was difficult and painful. And due to so many disappointments, I had become hard and bitter.

What does it mean to have childlike faith? The Lord led me to a book called, *Dancing with Snowmen: Restoring Childlike Faith to Adults Who Have Forgotten How to Have Fun with God* by Perry Stone.[122] I read this entire book in two days. I also listened to a teaching called *Childlike Faith* by Patricia King.[123] Children love to laugh, forgive easily, and simply believe. Children tell us honestly when we hurt their feelings. They don't hold their tears inside

---

[122] https://perrystone.org/product/dancing-with-snowmen-book/
[123] https://store.patriciakingministries.com/collections/audio/products/childlike-faith-for-grown-ups-3-cd?variant=733898905

but freely let them out. When they are done crying and the hurt is removed, they begin to laugh and play again. The hurt has already been forgotten.

Children dream big. What changes in us as adults to cause us to stop dreaming? The movie "Hook"[124] with Robin Williams is the story of a grown up Peter Pan who returns to Neverland to save his two children. Hook has kidnapped Peter's children and tries to turn them against their father. Peter has to relearn things he used to know. He has to overcome his adult negative thinking and learn how to have an imagination all over again. Peter Pan is an example of someone who needs his childlike faith restored. This is such a fun movie. We need to begin to imagine and dream big with wild abandon like a child.

Let's Rethink Image

People have told me over and over how unique I am. I've been told that the way I think and process is very different from other people. I am not sure if it was meant as a compliment or not, but I sure took it as one. When you hear the word image, what do you think of? Do you think of your physical, outward appearance? Do you think about what you look like when you look in a

---

[124] https://www.imdb.com/title/tt0102057/

mirror? Do you think of your reputation, or what others think about you? Do you think of a picture or work of art? Merriam-Webster defines "image" as a noun meaning, "1) visual representation of something; 2) a mental picture or impression of something; 3) a popular conception (as of a person, institution, or nation) projected especially through the mass media."[125]

We each have our own thoughts when it comes to image. Women tend to have physical image issues as they are constantly complaining about different parts of their bodies. Most women compare themselves with each other. There's not much we haven't heard. For example, I'm sure you've heard things like, "My eyes are too far apart. My eyes are too close together. I wish I had a different eye color. My legs are too thick. My legs are too thin. I'm too skinny. I'm too fat." Women with curly hair wish their hair was straight; those with straight hair wish for curly hair. We allow our culture to define what is and isn't beautiful. Is the beauty industry a higher authority of creation than God?

Satan has distorted the very definition of image. First, our Creator made every single one of us in His image, male and female.[126] Every human being holds a likeness

[125] https://www.merriam-webster.com/dictionary/image 2/7/2019
[126] Genesis 1:26

to God; therefore, when we criticize others or ourselves on physical appearance, we are criticizing God. Selah.

We were created in the very image of God; there is no one else like us. Have you ever put a puzzle together? I once saw a puzzle with 40,000 individual pieces. I cannot even comprehend the patience it would take to put that puzzle together. Imagine if that puzzle was in the form of a human being. I am using a human being because each believer contributes to create the ONE Body of Christ. What would happen if one of the puzzle pieces were missing? Remember the one that Jesus left the 99 in search of? The one the church didn't want? The puzzle would be incomplete without the one.

To have an incomplete puzzle would drive me absolutely, completely bonkers! I can't imagine doing all that work only to find one of the pieces missing. I would search everywhere until I found that missing puzzle piece. When that one piece was found, the puzzle can be completed. The puzzle isn't complete until ALL the pieces are in their place. We are each like a piece of a puzzle, unique and shaped differently. Are you one of the missing pieces to this present day puzzle? If so, are you ready to be found? Beloved, you are an important piece of God's puzzle. Only your unique piece can fit in the spot designated and reserved for you.

When we focus on the Creator, we please Him. He will take care of our image and reputation. But God, in His mercy, is more concerned about our spiritual, emotional, and physical health than He is about our reputations. He can repair reputations in a blink of an eye. He doesn't judge us based upon appearances, like people do. He genuinely cares about our hearts. God has created each one of us distinctively in His image. Next time you look in the mirror and critique your appearance, pause and remember that you are made in the image of God.

Mirror, Mirror on the wall
I'm made in God's image,
Simply Beyoutiful
And that is all.

PROCESS AND IMAGINATION
CHAPTER 25

I hear these questions often, "Why was I born?" What is my purpose for being alive?" There is something ingrained in us that longs to fulfill our purpose and make a difference in the world. These desires were placed inside of us not to bring frustration, but to draw us closer to our Creator and bring out our unique creative abilities.

First and foremost, God created us to have relationship with Him. Outside of that relationship, we will always feel like we are missing something. Nothing else can fill the void – not religion, other people, or material possessions. As we grow in relationship with Jesus, we find complete satisfaction and fulfillment, and ultimately, our life's purpose. The Apostle Paul said this,

> We have become his poetry, a re-created people that will fulfill the destiny he has given each of us, for we are joined to Jesus, the Anointed One. Even before we were born, God planned in advance our destiny

and the good works we would do to fulfill it![127]

The footnotes in the Passion Translation for the above verse say, "Our lives are the beautiful poetry written by God that will speak forth all that he desires in life. Although implied, these good works make up our destiny. As we yield to God, our prearranged destiny comes to pass and we are rewarded for simply doing what he wanted us to accomplish."[128] Jesus had a predetermined destiny for being on earth. Jesus prayed to the Father: "I glorified you on earth by completing down to the last detail what you assigned me to do."[129]

I actually pray this verse over my own life saying, "I thank You, Papa that I glorify you while I'm on this earth by completing down to the last detail everything you assigned me to do." I don't want any part of my destiny stolen because of my past, nor do I want any part of my destiny stolen because of fear. Jesus restores and reconciles us back to our rightful place through His blood. The path to get there may be longer than anticipated, but we will reach our destinations as we

---

[127] Ephesians 2:10 TPT

[128] https://www.biblegateway.com/passage/?search=Ephesians+2%3A10&version=TPT

[129] John 17:4 The Message

yield to Him. How exciting! (Insert cheerleader jumping up and down for you!)

Our destiny is often found in what we are passionate about. What gets you fired up? The thing that I am most passionate about is helping others who have been damaged by church culture. My heart yearns to see reformation in the church. I have great compassion for those who feel like misfits or outcasts in church society. How we approach the things we are passionate about matters. When we approach our passion through love, we offer solutions and create an atmosphere of unity. Let's face it. What the world needs now is love, sweet love.

On the surface, operating in love seems like a simple thing. Unfortunately, much of church culture is founded on fear, not love. For example, my husband and I needed some time together. We decided to take a long weekend, and we went to Atlanta to attend a Braves game. The baseball game happened to be on a Sunday. Outside the stadium there was a group of people passing out salvation flyers. If all they did was pass out flyers that would have been fine. But one guy went too far and told us that we were going to Hell because we were attending a baseball game instead of church. Seriously?! Apparently, he forgot that he wasn't in church either.

Sigh. He automatically assumed that we were heathens because we were attending a baseball game. I was completely repulsed and embarrassed. If that was the only representation of Jesus I had experienced, I wouldn't want Him. Who needs berated and condemned? No one. May God put a muzzle on our mouths to help us stay silent when our words are not filled with love.

Love is welcoming, not condemning. Sadly, many people have not experienced the accepting love of Jesus from Christians. Through my travels, I have found Believers who demonstrate the true love of Christ. I asked the Lord to help me love others like He does. Warning! I'm a hugger – the real, sincere hug. No "fake hugs" from me. #bearhug

One time while I was at the grocery store, I witnessed a woman ranting and storming off. I asked the Lord if I should approach her. Instead of judging her actions, I took the time to pause and listen. I felt a yes from the Holy Spirit. As she stomped down the aisle, I approached her and said, "Excuse me, ma'am, do you have a second?" She looked at me incredulous that I had stopped her; for a moment, I thought she was going to redirect her rage at me. But as she looked in my eyes, she slowly softened. I believe that she felt something, but didn't understand it. I told her I couldn't help noticing that she was upset and wanted to know if there was anything I could do to help her. Then, I asked if she would allow me to give her a hug. Her eyes widened, and she burst into a HUGE grin. I swear she really did. She opened her arms, and I engulfed her in a bear hug. When we finished hugging, she told me that was exactly what she needed; everything was going wrong for her that day.

Seems simple, doesn't it? A hug. As I hugged her, I silently said a prayer for her. I know she felt God's love pour out of me. As God heals us, then we can become the person that we needed when we felt broken. That's all I'm doing – being the person I needed for others in the same situations.

As God fills in our broken places with His love, we gain the confidence to be who God created us to be. We never have to apologize to anyone for being ourselves, or for doing what we are called and created to do. Don't worry if it's outside the religious box because Jesus can't be put in a box. Simply do what God lays on your heart to do, keeping in mind that God's ideas always revolve around faith, hope, and love.

Born to Create

Have you ever heard the famous Dr. Seuss quote, "Why

fit in when you were born to stand out!"?[130] Why do we struggle to fit into a manmade mold? Insecurity plagues us because of society's standards. We try to blend in and be like everyone else. We tend to care more about what people think than what God thinks. Afraid of criticism, we strive to either keep up with the Jones' or create an image that avoids attention. The truth is there will always be someone critiquing us.

As we grow in the knowledge of who we are and Whose we are, we begin to walk freely in our uniqueness and confidently in our personality. Why imitate someone else when the world needs YOU to be who you are? We've all heard it said that imitation is the sincerest form of flattery. No! That's a lie! Imitation is a counterfeit of who we were designed to be. Imitation is the counterfeit of image and imagination.

We were born to create. God is a creator; He placed His creative nature inside of us. Take a moment and think about creation. The landscape of the earth is filled with breathtaking mountains, oceans, deserts, and lush green fields. Outside the realm of the earth are the sun, moon, and stars. Take a minute to think about the various shapes and colors. No two snowflakes are the same. God

---

[130] https://www.goodreads.com/quotes/187115-why-fit-in-when-you-were-born-to-stand-out

loves diversity! Even identical twins have uniqueness all their own.

God planted longings and dreams in our hearts for a purpose. He desires for our creativity to be unleashed so that we bring Him glory. We have allowed society and religion to dictate how we should think, feel, and act. God's Word is solid truth and never changes, but we have a limited understanding of the scripture. The devil wants to keep the Church deceived thinking they have to look and act like everyone else. He is terrified of God's children tapping into the creative power of God as it will wreak havoc in the kingdom of darkness.

Power of Process

Comparison is a dream killer. God made us uniquely beautiful, and our journeys look different. There is a lot that goes on that is not seen by others. I call this the "Power of Process." Celebrate with others when they reach their dreams! Be encouraged that you have what it takes to reach yours as well. Don't quit in difficult places.

When you look at a flower, do you consider all the stages the flower went through before reaching full bloom? No, we look at the flower and only see its beauty. We may admire different shades of color in a bouquet. We may even put our noses close to the petals and inhale the fragrance. Nevertheless, in order for us to enjoy the flower, it has to go through a process. It starts out as a seed, planted in good soil. The seed needs water, nutrients, and sunlight. The seed then takes root and develops a food store. Then, a shoot sprouts from the food store peeking through the dirt. Finally, the stem, leaves, seed pod, and petals are seen.

Our dreams are like seeds planted in the soil of our hearts. The things needed to make our dreams grow are in the power of process. We have to till the soil of our soul to ensure that there are no roots of bitterness to choke and kill our dreams. We also need to weed our hearts of things like insecurity, unforgiveness, shame, fear, etc. Jesus is the sunlight, the Holy Spirit is the water, and the food store is the Word of God, all providing nutrients necessary to enable our dreams to grow. How do we make the garden of our heart healthy, and the seeds of our dreams grow? How do we get the fruit of our garden ready for harvest?

As we begin to prepare the soil of our hearts, people will begin to see changes in us. Just like with a garden, when you clear the soil of the weeds, you are able to see the baby sprouts. Mature flowers have deep roots. As we grow healthier and more mature, our roots will deepen.

We will begin to display the characteristics of the fruit of the Spirit.[131] The point of the growth process is to enable us to handle the manifestation of the dream.

ROCKY

I used to love watching the Rocky movies with my dad. As we watched the final fight, we would pretend to be in the ring with Rocky, throwing fake punches in the air. Rocky Balboa has inspired me on so many levels. In the original Rocky movie, Rocky is "a small-time boxer gets a supremely rare chance to fight a heavy-weight champion in a bout in which he strives to go the distance for his self-respect."[132] Spoiler alert: Rocky loses in the end by a technical decision. In Rocky II, "Rocky struggles in family life after his bout with Apollo Creed, while the embarrassed champ insistently goads him to accept a challenge for a rematch."[133]

Rocky III starts with the Italian Stallion so famous that his likeness is everywhere, including pinball machines. Fame and complacency soon cause Balboa to lose his title to young thug Clubber Lang, who inadvertently causes the death of Rocky's

---

[131] Galatians 5:22-26
[132] https://www.imdb.com/title/tt0075148/
[133] https://www.imdb.com/title/tt0079817/

beloved trainer, Mickey, before their first championship bout. After sinking into a depression, Balboa must regain the love and support of his family, as well as the elusive "eye of the tiger," the hungry need to beat the opponent which former foe Apollo Creed teaches him during this film's training sequence. In the end, Balboa faces off against Lang for a second time.[134]

In Rocky III, Rocky confesses for the first time in his life he is afraid. Rocky had to fight the battle in his mind before he could fight it in the ring. Rocky had two choices: 1) He could allow defeat to carry him further into his pain, and regret would eat him alive for the rest of his life; or 2) He could face the battle in his mind, stand up to the fear in his heart, and face his fear in the ring for another match. Spoiler alert: Rocky reclaims the heavy weight title at the end of the movie.

We could continue with Rocky IV, but you get the picture. The Rocky movies are a great visual of someone who had a dream. He obtained his dream, but he wasn't mature enough to handle the fame that came with it. We observe him as he battles defeat, shame, and fear. We watch as he overcomes these internal strongholds to empower the

---

[134] https://www.imdb.com/title/tt0084602/

champion within to emerge once again. The power of process is necessary to get from point A, the dream, to point B, the manifestation of the dream.

Power of Pure Imagination

I have always had an outrageous imagination. I would dream big and share my dreams with my family growing up. They would laugh and indulge me because it was entertaining. Kids are not shy about their imaginations. There is a world created that brings wonder and joy.

Did you ever watch Willy Wonka & the Chocolate Factory, the original version with Gene Wilder? The general storyline is this:

> The world is astounded when Willy Wonka, for years a recluse in his factory, announces that five lucky people will be given a tour of the factory, shown all the secrets of his amazing candy, and one will win a lifetime supply of Wonka chocolate. Nobody wants the prize more than young Charlie, but as his family is so poor that buying even one bar of chocolate is a treat, buying enough bars to find one of the five golden tickets is unlikely in the extreme. But in movieland, magic can happen.

Charlie, along with four somewhat odious other children, get the chance of a lifetime and a tour of the factory. Along the way, mild disasters befall each of the odious children, but can Charlie beat the odds and grab the brass ring?[135]

These children were allowed to bring one adult with them. As the winners enter one of the first rooms, Willy Wonka said, "Inside this room, all of my dreams become realities, and some of my realities become dreams. And, almost everything you'll see is eatable, edible, I mean, you can eat almost everything."[136] This room had a chocolate river and a candy garden. Everything in the room was literally edible. The children's reactions in the film regarding this room were authentic. They had not seen the room before filming. Such fun![137]

During this scene, Willy Wonka plucks a yellow teacup and saucer from a plant and begins to drink from it. He then takes a bite of the cup. He sings the song, "Pure Imagination," it goes like this:

---

[135] https://www.imdb.com/title/tt0067992/
[136] http://www.moviequotes.com/fullquote.cgi?qnum=1545
[137]
https://www.imdb.com/title/tt0067992/trivia?ref_=tt_trv_trv%C3%A
7

If you want to view paradise
Simply look around and view it
Anything you want to, do it
Wanta change the world?
There's nothing to it

There is no life I know
To compare with pure imagination
Living there, you'll be free
If you truly wish to be[138]

If we didn't have imaginations, how would we see images in our minds and receive impressions? As you read the story about the chocolate room, did you get impressions in your mind? That's vision. In the last chapter, we talked about being made in the image of God. He used His imagination to create the world and everything in it. We are created in His image with the power to create. If we can imagine it, we can create it.

Remember the story about Mary Lou Retton? She imagined herself with the gold medal. That's the power of imagination. Rocky saw himself as a champion, and then he was able to defeat his opponent.

138

https://www.stlyrics.com/lyrics/willywonkaandthechocolatefactory/pureimagination.htm

If you can see it, you can achieve it. This is why Vision Boards have become very popular. People are beginning to understand the power of envisioning their dreams so that they can make them a reality.

As the Lord and I have journeyed together, my vision changed. The pictures in my mind changed. The vision I had of myself began to change. I didn't see myself any longer as what others said about me. Instead, I began to believe what God said about me, and the images in my mind began to transform. This is what brings freedom. For example, when I was reading Psalm 23, I began to see pictures of the Lord and I walking beside the still waters. This is pure imagination. Does that mean it's not real? No, it is very real. There is a natural realm and a spiritual realm; I was engaging in both realms.

Does your imagination need to be healed from trauma? Is your imagination constantly revisiting hurtful and painful places from your past? Satan tries to use our imaginations against us to keep us in bondage, so we cannot dream and enter our destiny. He is clever and crafty, but as you understand his tactics, you can begin to fight back and gain healing. There is something so indescribably amazing about a pure imagination. Pure imagination is a playground for our childlike faith!

SIMPLY BEYOUTIFUL

CHAPTER 26

There is nothing more painful than dealing with the pain of toxic Christianity. When we need answers but only find more questions, it can be quite troubling. But God is faithful! He has the balm for our heartache, solutions to our issues, and answers for our questions. I've shared some very personal stories and given you a glimpse of how God has healed me from the damage done through trauma and toxic Christianity. He really does give us beauty for ashes!

What is beauty? Merriam-Webster defines beauty as a noun meaning, "the quality or aggregate of qualities in a person or thing that gives pleasure to the senses or pleasurably exalts the mind or spirit : loveliness."[139] God has been highlighting the words beautiful and beauty to me. One day I received a bouquet of roses with Song of Solomon 4:7 written on the card, "You are altogether beautiful, my darling; there is no flaw in you." Tears welled up in my eyes as God reminded me how beautiful

---

[139] https://www.merriam-webster.com/dictionary/beauty

I am; He didn't see any flaws in me. Even with my colorful past, even with my emotional scars, God doesn't see flaws in me. Guess what? He doesn't see flaws in you either. The blood of Jesus covers and washes away every imperfection in us. God sees us pure, holy, and all-together beautiful.

During prayer one evening, God spoke tenderly to my heart, and I felt like He wanted me to put what I had heard in this book. May His words heal your heart as it did mine.

I created your beauty, daughter, for My pleasure. It is to bring glory to Me on this earth. You have been attacked in this area because the enemy doesn't want your beauty to shine! You have been purified through fire, so your beauty brings Me glory! You are on your final path to freedom! No more will you hide and be bound by being overweight. For I am placing in you My confidence, and you will no longer take it lightly or give it up freely.

As a master carver carves the stone, piece by piece, I have carved you, My beloved daughter. Piece by piece, I have created you, the perfect masterpiece for such a time as this. You are a delight to Me when you laugh and I see you enjoy your day. I love to see you celebrate the colors that I have made not worrying about what others think. I have placed this love in you for colors....

Rest and enjoy as I work on your behalf. I am well pleased with you, daughter, because you have yielded to Me. Even though at times you wanted to shrink away, you always turned back to Me. Even my disciples had character flaws and made mistakes, yet I used them for My glory as I will use you for My glory.

God loves to confirm His word to us. I went on a spiritual business trip to Costa Rica facilitated by Donna Partow and Tamara Aragon which was designed to show me how to pursue my dreams. Tamara and I had not met before the trip, nor had we discussed what God was speaking to me. She shared Isaiah 62:3 with me, "You shall be a crown of beauty (glory) in the hand of the LORD, and a royal diadem in the hand of your God."[140] Soon after I returned from Costa Rica, my daughter gave me a Bath & Body Works gift set titled, "Hello Beautiful." Really!?! These are just a couple of the ways that God was spotlighting the words beauty and beautiful to me. Y'all

---

[140] Isaiah 62:3 ESV

this is fun living; it feels like a treasure hunt! Who doesn't want to find a treasure chest filled with gold and precious jewels? The greatest treasure is the wisdom, revelation, and understanding we receive from the Lord. It is this treasure that empowers us to live abundantly. King Solomon said this:

> For if you keep seeking it like a man would seek for sterling silver, searching in hidden places for cherished treasure, then you will discover the fear of the Lord and find the true knowledge of God. Wisdom is a gift from a generous God, and every word he speaks is full of revelation and becomes a fountain of understanding within you. For the Lord has a hidden storehouse of wisdom made accessible to his godly lovers. He becomes your personal bodyguard as you follow his ways, protecting and guarding you as you choose what is right.[141]

Why does God say things but the meaning is not immediately clear? Why does He ask us to search for understanding? I used to get so frustrated with God. I once told Him, "If you have something to say, shoot straight with me, and say what You mean." Rather than

---

[141] Proverbs 2:4-8 TPT

rebuking me for my annoyance, He gently whispered, "The most precious revelation that I have to give is for My bride. It is only in the place of intimacy that I reveal My heart for my beloved." Then I felt led to read Matthew 7:6-8,

> Who would hang earrings on a dog's ear or throw pearls in front of wild pigs? They'll only trample them under their feet and then turn around and tear you to pieces! "Ask, and the gift is yours. Seek, and you'll discover. Knock, and the door will be opened for you. For every persistent one will get what he asks for. Every persistent seeker will discover what he longs for. And everyone who knocks persistently will one day find an open door.[142]

The Passion Translation includes a footnote for verse six. It says,

> The Aramaic word for "earrings" is almost identical to the word for "holy." Earrings and pearls are symbols of spiritual truths given to us by God. They give us beautiful "ears" to hear his voice and impart lovely pearls of wisdom, which are not to be

---

[142] Matthew 7:6-8 TPT

regarded lightly or shared with those who have their hearts closed. The Aramaic word for "throw" is almost identical to the word for "to instruct" or "to teach." The value of wisdom is not appreciated by those who have no ears to hear it.[143]

When we seek to gain a more clear understanding of something, we are searching for buried treasure. As we seek God, we will find Him. The amazing thing is that God will always lead us to where X marks the spot. God isn't afraid of our questions. In fact, He welcomes them. He doesn't get upset with our frustration or lack of understanding. He doesn't berate or belittle us; rather, He leads us down a path of discovery.

What I discovered about beauty is that it equates with glory! "Bold power and glorious majesty are wrapped around her as she laughs with joy over the latter days."[144] Beloved, God's definition of beauty and the world's definition are two different things. True beauty shines from within. There is an original "you" that God designed before the pain, before the trauma, before the lies. Oh Beautiful One, God's strategic plan allows for broken

---

143
https://www.biblegateway.com/passage/?search=Matthew+7%3A6-8&version=TPT
[144] Proverbs 31:25 TPT

pieces. His plan wasn't to hurt or harm you. His plan wasn't for your pain. His plan is for you to know Him and the power of His resurrection.

It's time to arise and awaken! It's time to shed the grave clothes that others have wrapped around us. Jesus didn't die for us to continually live in shame and condemnation. He didn't grab the keys to the devil's house for us to rent a room there. No, He endured the cross and conquered the grave to go and prepare a place for us! God wants to fill us with His glory, His beauty. God wants us to carry an anointing of glory that shifts the atmosphere wherever we go – whether it's work, the grocery store, the gas station, etc. Wherever we are, God desires to display His majesty and glory through us.

As we allow Him to mend our hearts, the light of our souls overcomes the darkness of our past. The wounds of our past no longer serve as a hindrance to stop the love and beauty of God from flowing out of us. The Apostle Paul said,

> We can all draw close to him with the veil removed from our faces. And with no veil we all become like mirrors who brightly **reflect the glory of the Lord Jesus**. We are being transfigured into his very image as we move from one brighter level of

glory to another. And this glorious transfiguration comes from the Lord, who is the Spirit.[145] (Emphasis added)

We are transformed into the SAME IMAGE from GLORY to GLORY as by the Spirit of the Lord. An authentic, true believer in Jesus Christ transmits glory! The Apostle Paul prayed,

I pray that the **Father of glory**, the God of our Lord Jesus Christ, would impart to you the riches of the Spirit of wisdom and the Spirit of revelation to know him through your deepening intimacy with him.

I pray that the light of God will **illuminate the eyes of your imagination**, flooding you with light, until you **experience the full revelation of the hope of his calling**—that is, the wealth of God's glorious inheritances that he finds in us, his holy ones!

I pray that you will continually experience the immeasurable greatness of **God's power made available to you through faith. Then your lives will be an advertisement of this immense power**

---

[145] 2 Corinthians 3:18 TPT

as it works through you! This is the mighty power that was released when God raised Christ from the dead and exalted him to the place of highest honor and supreme authority in the heavenly realm![146] (Emphasis added)

He is our Father of Glory! Satan doesn't want us to really know God because of the glory, the beauty that will shine forth through us. Satan will do everything in his power to keep us believing lies – including causing experiences that reinforce those lies. Why? Because we are sons and daughters of GLORY. We are glory carriers through Christ.

Your natural talents are supernatural to someone who doesn't have the same talents. Your talents are part of God's glory to benefit those around you. Your quirks are nothing to be ashamed of because they are for a purpose. Your personality combined with your idiosyncrasies and talents make you one of a kind. You are irreplaceable. God put a unique piece of His Glory inside of you. There is a big picture. You are one piece of the puzzle that is distinctively designed to fit into God's plan; a glory carrier in the big picture.

---

[146] Ephesians 1:17-20 TPT

You have a decision to make. You can choose to take the proverbial blue pill. Go back to bed. When you wake up, you can keep seeing the world as you currently do. OR, you can choose to take the proverbial red pill. You can go on this grand adventure, this treasure hunt with God to every broken and hidden place deep within your heart. Oh, but when these broken places are mended, He will illuminate within you the beautifully rich treasure He has placed inside of you. Then, you will move forward with confidence and glory, find people who celebrate one another, and together you will demonstrate God's love to the world around you.

Will you allow God to heal you of all your negative experiences with toxic Christians? Will you allow Him to show you who you really are? Will you allow Him to show you who He really is? I promise that you will never regret the journey. As you allow the Holy Spirit to gently put back together every broken piece of your soul, your original masterpiece will come forth in glorious, beautiful majesty. You will be able to laugh with joy and make Satan sorry he ever messed with you! Beloved, you are God's beautiful, unique masterpiece. You were created for such a time as this! Go forth! Choose to be a son or daughter of glory!

Be you.

Be beautiful.

Simply BeYOUtiful!

Arise [from the depression and prostration in which circumstances have kept you—rise to a new life]! Shine (be radiant with the glory of the Lord), for your light has come, and the glory of the Lord has risen upon you![147]

---

[147] Isaiah 60:1 AMPC

ABOUT THE AUTHOR

Shannon D. Hair is an author, speaker, and certified deep inner healing and deliverance minister. Called a FREEDOM-BRINGER, she specializes in helping others overcome their traumatic past and bring them back to their TRUE LOVE, JESUS!

Her life passion is to partner with Jesus to see many people step into the highest level of freedom possible.

Shannon has a shepherd's heart to also teach the whole counsel of the Word of God by exposing the lies of the enemy and expressing God's unfailing love!

Through her gifting, she desires to establish a safe haven for those hungry for the Presence of God. She communicates with authenticity and authority by bringing her unique ability to speak directly in love, comfort, and encouragement while adding humor into difficult and painful places of the soul!

www.simplyshannon.org

PAY IT FORWARD

I'm absolutely thrilled that you took the time to read my book. I hope it brought you blessings and inspiration.

Now, I have a humble request that would mean the world to me. Could you please spare a moment to help others discover the transformative power of *Simply Be*YOU*tiful!* by writing a review?

Your words, straight from the heart, hold immense value. Your contribution can make a significant impact on the lives of those who come across the book.

Thank you so much for being part of the journey to share these transformative ideas with others.

Go to: www.amazon.com/review/create-review.

Ever wondered how to activate your prophetic words to unlock the incredible goodness of God?

Ever wondered what to do with a prophetic word?

Join Shannon on an extraordinary journey as she unveils her remarkable 10 step plan, meticulously crafted to unlock the fullness of God's plans for you. But this isn't just a mere roadmap; it's a heartfelt revelation of Shannon's own encounters with God's transformative power.

Delve into the pages of this book and be captivated by the stories of miracles, breakthroughs, and unexpected blessings that will ignite your faith.

If God did it for her, He will do it for you!

www.simplyshannon.org

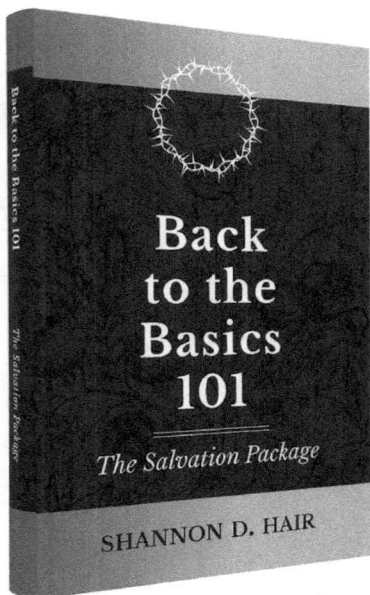

Did you know that salvation is so much more than just staying out of hell or going to heaven?

Does the false represent-ation of Jesus make you want to run FROM Him instead of TO Him?

Whether you process things logically or emotionally, this book will speak directly to you. Shannon D, Hair will take you on an eye-opening journey in a very practical way to show you just how valuable you are and the price that Jesus willingly paid because of His great love for you. Learn what salvation really means and everything included in the salvation package.

Salvation is just the beginning. It's a beautiful divine romance. Led by love, you will know with certainty what you believe and why you believe it! Be ready to laugh and cry as the yearning in your heart is answered within these pages.

www.simplyshannon.org